Surf, Sand & Streetcars

A Mobile History of Santa Cruz, California

Charles S. McCaleb

Interurbans Special 67

Surf, Sand & Streetcars

Library of Congress Catalog Number 77-014900
ISBN: 0-916374-28-9

First Printing: Fall 1977

Interurbans

P.O. Box 6444
Glendale, California 91205

Publisher . . . . Mac Sebree
Editor . . . . .Jim Walker

Dust Jacket Photograph

ONE OF SANTA CRUZ'S HANDSOME electric cars pauses among the tall trees at Twin Lakes for an early-day photographer to capture the crew on film. At left is the conductor; next to him holding the controller handle is the moustachioed motorman.
Randolph Brandt Collection

Title Page Photo

IT IS 1916 in downtown Santa Cruz, and Union Traction No. 11 rumbles southbound on Pacific Avenue past the I.O.O.F. town-clock building. Although nothing but "flivvers" are parked on the street, a hitching post is still in place on the curb to the right side. The horse-and-buggy era was not that long dead.
UCSC, Preston Sawyer Collection

Dedicated to my wife Joy, who has helped in countless ways with the preparation of this book.

Table of Contents

Preface

HORSECARS operated in Santa Cruz, on California's central coast, from August 1875 to July 1910. Electric streetcars ran from November 1891 to January 1926, when the last cars were retired in favor of motor coaches. Sometimes there was only one local streetcar company. Often there were two. Once there were three. That was from November 1891 to August 1892, when one horsecar company held sway in Pacific Avenue, another in Soquel Road, and the city's first electric cars ran from Garfield Park to the beach by a tortuous route. Eventually all operations were consolidated in one company—Union Traction—but not before years of wrangling that involved some of the most colorful and engaging personalities ever to light the Santa Cruz scene.

To Frederick A. Hihn, the indomitable German who fashioned a fortune from the ashes of a ruined business, go the laurels for building the city's first horsecar line. James P. Pierce, the Santa Clara lumberman, came to challenge him and stayed long after Hihn quit the fray. Thomas Cole, the mining man, succeeded Pierce and gave way in turn to Anson P. Hotaling, the San Francisco merchant prince. Local capitalist William Ely built the city's first interurban horsecar line—to East Santa Cruz, Twin Lakes, and Arana Gulch—on the very eve of electric streetcars.

Honors for the first electrics go jointly to James Philip Smith, the New York and Paris businessman, and to Fred W. Swanton, the flamboyant promoter of local utilities, streetcars, and the Santa Cruz Seaside Company. Swanton is a study unto himself. Next came a parade of high-rolling adventurers, among them James

W. Forgeus, F.S. Granger, and John M. Gardiner, who took charge briefly, expanded the streetcar systems, and used them as pawns in financial games involving millions. Finally there were John Martin, co-founder of Pacific Gas and Electric Company, and S. Waldo Coleman, who completed the development and administered Union Traction to the end.

This story—a chronicle of these men and others, set against a backdrop of five decades of Santa Cruz life—is contained among entries in a 193-page working notebook now property of the Santa Cruz Public Library. Data are from county and city records, files of the state's Public Utilities Commission, newspaper accounts, reference documents, and, in a few cases, personal recollections.

Photographs—individually credited—are from Randolph (Rudy) Brandt and Charles Smallwood of San Francisco; Vernon Sappers of Oakland; Hal Van Gorder, Warren Littlefield, Noel Patterson, Alberta McCormick, and Margaret Koch of Santa Cruz; Lewis V. Coleman of Woodside; Nancy Lucking Sedon of Berkeley; William Wulf of Los Gatos; Roger Ciapponi of Fremont; Pacific Gas and Electric Company; San Jose Public Library; and University of California-Santa Cruz (the Preston Sawyer Collection). Where possible they are credited to original sources. My son, Donald C. McCaleb of Palo Alto, helped with the research. Mr. Brandt, Mr. Smallwood, and James K. Gibson of San Francisco helped with the equipment rosters. To all, and to the staff of the *Santa Cruz Sentinel*, I express my thanks.

CHARLES S. MCCALEB
San Jose, California

BIRD'S-EYE VIEW of Santa Cruz in the early 1870s, before building of the Santa Cruz Railroad. Nearly 200 years ago the city and county began with the establishment of Mission Santa Cruz (Holy Cross in Spanish) by Father Junipero Serra.

UCSC, Preston Sawyer Collection

EARLY VIEW OF LOWER PLAZA when businesses were building "down on the flat." The date is about 1860; Hugo Hihn's Flatiron Building (center) is just completed. Left foreground is part of Elihu Anthony's building, the first built on the flat. Beyond it is Santa Cruz House (story and a half) and beyond that Franklin House, saloons, and Chinese laundries reaching down First Street. Lower right foreground is Charles D. Eldon's store and beyond that lies Frederick A. Hihn's store.

UCSC, Preston Sawyer Collection

Part 1

Horsecar Era

ON A MIDSUMMER morning in 1875, Santa Cruz's first horsecar stood waiting in the Lower Plaza, Pacific Avenue and Front Street, ready to set out for the beachfront two miles away.

This was a moment long awaited by the community. Gathered for the occasion were townspeople, merchants, and officials of the narrow-gauge Santa Cruz steam railroad, promoters also of the horsecar line. Among these were Titus Hale, Benjamin F. Porter, and capitalist Frederick Augustus Hihn, pioneering businessman, lumberman, and developer of the nearby Camp Capitola beachside resort.

In the Plaza, decked out for opening day, was a little red narrow-gauge car "painted and lettered by Mr. Bowman, a resident workman. The job is a very fine one," commended the *Santa Cruz Sentinel*, "and reflects credit on Mr. B." Dignitaries climbed aboard. Promptly at 11 o'clock the car hauled westward into Mission Street, swung briefly into Vine Street (now Center Street), and continued out Cherry and Rincon Streets (both now Chestnut) to the newly laid tracks of the *Santa Cruz Railroad*, which were not yet in service in

Santa Cruz. Here a switch allowed the horsecar to enter the railroad. Onward plodded the little car down Chestnut Street through a cut in Beach Hill to the wharf area, where the tracks turned eastward along the beach. It reined to a halt at Leibbrandt's bathhouse, the line's waterfront terminus.

The date of this run was August 3, 1875. The trip took about 30 minutes. Regular service commenced that afternoon and was acclaimed a success, a thousand tickets being sold in just three days. Reported the *Sentinel:* "The time-table on the street cars will soon be established and published for the information of the public. Twenty-five cents will purchase four street car tickets, or the price for nine is fifty cents. The street cars will run to the beach to-night (August 7), to accommodate those who desire to attend the dance at Leibbrandt's."

A second car soon was added to the line. Within the month, horsecars were making 10 trips daily from the Lower Plaza to the beach, and the promoters allowed as how their new enterprise was a "paying business."

THIS RARE photograph possibly is the only existing picture of a Hihn "Red Line" horsecar and may even have been taken August 3, 1875, when the company inaugurated service from the Lower Plaza to the beach.
William Wulf Collection

1. Wave of Prosperity

HORSECARS had come to Santa Cruz on a "wave of prosperity so general that we find new buildings going up on every street." Santa Cruz was booming, and the *Sentinel* could hardly contain its enthusiasm. The community, located on the shores of Monterey Bar near the Santa Cruz Mountains about 75 miles south of San Francisco, now counted a population exceeding 4,500. Resort and retail businesses, mostly on the flats in and around the Lower Plaza, were flourishing. Plans were pending for a town water system, a cement plant, and a flour mill (the famous Centennial Mill of 1876). Property values were climbing briskly as the Santa Cruz Railroad pressed toward a junction with the Southern Pacific at Pajaro, near Watsonville about 20 miles southeast of Santa Cruz. That would open the community by rail to the rest of the nation. Rumor spoke of a second rail company preparing to build down the Pacific Coast from San Francisco to Santa Cruz. Now under construction was yet another: a seven-mile, narrow-gauge logging pike (the Santa Cruz and Felton) that twisted up into the mountains along the west bank of the San Lorenzo River—this road expected to be in operation by year's end.

SANTA CRUZ FOUNDRY on River Street reportedly made parts for Santa Cruz Railroad, Hihn's horsecar company, and probably William Ely's East Santa Cruz horse railroad. *Harold Van Gorder Collection*

This flurry of local railroad building was an outgrowth of activities begun in the 1850s. Americans drawn to the area after California achieved statehood found arable plains and plentiful resources waiting to be developed if transportation were available. So they built wharves, improved the roads, founded steamer and stage lines, and prepared for the growth to come. And come it did. Coastal steamers now put in regularly to Santa Cruz delivering finished products and taking on lumber, lime, leather, and blasting powder (an important local export). By steamer and stage came vacationers attracted by Santa Cruz's equable climate and several resorts of widening fame, including Camp Capitola to the east and the Pacific Ocean House, St. Charles Hotel, and Pope House in Santa Cruz itself. The St. Charles, in the Lower Plaza, modestly called itself "the finest and best run first-class hotel outside of San Francisco." Pope House, a cottage resort up Mission Hill, was just commencing four decades as a favored gathering place for San Francisco's wealthy and social elite, who would bring their ornate barouches and phaetons, their carriage horses and servants, to enliven the Santa Cruz summers.

Many men were responsible for these developments but chief among them was Frederick A. Hihn, the sturdy German emigrant who dominated local history from his arrival in Santa Cruz (October 1851) until

FREDERICK A. HIHN. This photograph is dated November 24, 1892. *Courtesy Noel Patterson*

about the turn of the century. It was Hihn who not only laid out plans for the Santa Cruz-Watsonville coastal railway and the Santa Cruz-Felton logging road but also, as a state assemblyman, helped pass the legislation that permitted California counties to finance railroad construction, thus making possible the two roads. It was he who secured first rights for a horsecar operation in Santa Cruz, from the California State Legislature in March 1872, for a line down the west bank of the San Lorenzo from the Lower Plaza to the beach. (This line was never built.) Hihn was a visionary who could rally public support behind his causes. He was also an eminently practical man who profited well from his ventures and became Santa Cruz's wealthiest citizen, the founder of several industries and a thriving real estate business. It is said that Hihn once owned a sixth of all the land in the Santa Cruz County and had mortgages on much of the rest.

(ABOVE) HIHN RESIDENCE. This stately mansion was for years a Santa Cruz landmark.
Harold Van Gorder Collection

2. Steam Trains and Streetcars

HIHN CAME to Santa Cruz a young man pursued by misfortune. Born 1829 in Holzminden, Germany, he emigrated to California around the Horn in 1849 seeking gold in the Sierras. Flooded out by the Feather River, where he lived briefly on manzanita berries, he retreated to Sacramento, where he and a partner set up a candy factory. Flood waters from the Sacramento and American Rivers put him out of business again.

Hihn next worked the mines at Long Bar, near Auburn, earning a stake with which he bought a hotel interest in Sacramento. But business was slow, so he sold out and went to San Francisco and opened a drug store.

There, the catastrophic fire of 1851 burned him out. In desperation he made plans to return to Germany. But while making his way to the waterfront, he passed a friend rooting around in the ashes of his own burned-out business. Learning that the friend planned to rebuild, Hihn took hope and formed a partnership with Henry Hintch that led to a general merchandising business in Santa Cruz at Pacific Avenue and Front Street. By 1857 Hihn had prospered and sold this business to his brother Hugo, who in 1860 built the flatiron building that still stands in the mid-1970s at the corner of Pacific and Front.

The sturdy German was now an important property owner and community leader who had helped build the first Capitola wharf (1857) and the first toll road over the mountains to the Santa Clara Valley (1858). In the 1860s he added substantially to his holdings, coming to ownership of large tracts of marketable timber and also the Soquel Augmentation Rancho where in 1869, along the bay shore, he laid out his Camp Capitola resort along the lines of European watering places. By the end of the decade he owned sawmills, other businesses, and properties on almost every street of Santa Cruz.

It was the Camp Capitola project and Hihn's need for cheap, large-volume lumber shipments that stimulated his interest in a Santa Cruz-Felton logging road (1871) and the Santa Cruz-Watsonville coastal railway (1866). The latter was his most ambitious project. He first planned to entice the Southern Pacific into building the line by offering a county subsidy. The scheme won countrywide support, but the Southern Pacific ignored the bait. Then the Southern Pacific opened in November 1871 to Pajaro, where a connection could be made. And German-born Claus Spreckels, California's legendary Sugar King, bought nearby Rancho Aptos and decided to build a resort patterned after Camp Capitola. Hihn and Spreckels formed an alliance to build the railroad themselves, and again won a county subsidy despite some local opposition. That led in June 1873 to formation of the *Santa Cruz Railroad,* its directorate consisting of Hihn and Spreckels (the majority stockholders), Titus Hale, Benjamin Porter, and Amasa

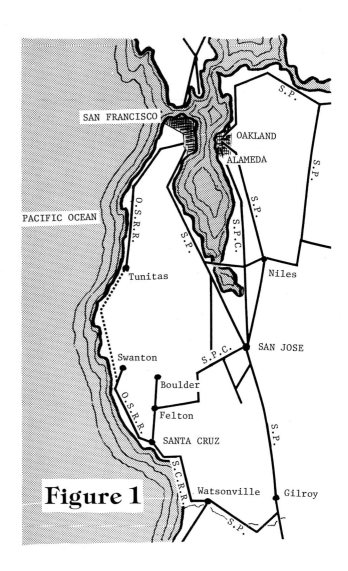

Figure 1

Railroad Names:
O.S.R.R. — Ocean Shore Railroad
S.C.R.R. — Santa Cruz Railroad
S.P.C. — South Pacific Coast
S.P. — Southern Pacific

Pray, American-born merchant and town trustee called by the *Sentinel* "one of the oldest residents and heaviest men in the county." Hale was Spreckels' manager at Aptos. Porter, owner of a local tannery, was well respected in Santa Cruz business circles.

Construction went slowly. In December 1874, having finished five miles of track, the railroad ran a short excursion from the east bank of the San Lorenzo River, its terminus at that time. Still to be confirmed was its route through Santa Cruz. On February 3, 1875, the town fathers resolved this matter by granting rights across the San Lorenzo, along the beach, and across Pacific Avenue and Bay Street through the lands of Harriet Mead Blackburn into Chestnut Street, thence to a terminus at Rincon and Green Streets. The franchise specified iron T-rail and a maximum speed of eight miles per hour. The railroad was required to lay macadam or planking between the rails and two feet on each side. Also specified was a minimum three-foot gauge, which the railroad adopted.

Supporting Hihn and Spreckels' petition for a franchise were 24 property owners including Mrs. Blackburn (widow of the late judge), realtor Thomas J. Weeks, and German-born harnessmaker John Werner, friend and associate of Hihn.

Also awarded by the town fathers that day was a street railroad franchise to Hale, Spreckels, Porter, and associates stipulating a maximum fare of 6¼¢ and the Mission-Vine-Cherry-Chestnut route from the Lower Plaza to the beach, terminating on the San Lorenzo east bank. This represented an evolution in Hihn's thinking. Not only could he make dual use of the steam railroad tracks for steam trains and streetcars, but the horsecar service would promote land values along Chestnut Street, where he and others owned considerable property. It was a useful plum to dangle before the town fathers who, tired of the dusty streets that became quagmires during the winter rains, wholeheartedly supported the project.

During spring and summer of 1875, the steam railroad began regular service incrementally from the San Lorenzo east bank (on May 16, for example, to Aptos). Under construction was a 550-foot bridge over the San Lorenzo. In Santa Cruz arrived ties, ballast, and rails not only for the steam railroad but also for the horse railroad, plus two horsecars. "The streets are almost constantly blockaded," chided the *Sentinel*. "Building materials, teams, and Chinamen on the new horse-car tracks do the business. Hurry up, friends, and clear the way."

By August the way was indeed clear and horsecar service began. Protected from steam trains by the unfinished bridge, the cars of Hihn's "red line"—as it came to be called—made safe headway to and from the beach on regular schedules. But the day was fast approaching when the "red line" steeds would meet those of a different nature, with unpredictable results. That day came Sunday, May 7, 1876, when the 22-ton locomotive *Jupiter* swept across the bridge dragging a diminutive passenger coach. The *Sentinel's* editor waxed eloquent for the occasion:

> "At last our enterprising young city is in full connection with the rest of mankind. At last she is free from the rule of the sleepy stage coach. At last she is counted among the shining jewels that the deft fingers of commerce have woven together with threads of iron. At last the same conduit of life and wealth that vivifies her sister cities brings daily treasures to the veins of Santa Cruz.
>
> "Such in substance was the proclamation sent forth upon the triumphant shout of the dashing young steed which, fresh from his birthplace beyond the Sierras, crossed the Pajaro River the other day and came speeding down the track of the Santa Cruz Railroad, bringing with him a dainty and elegant chariot fit for the conveyance of the most fastidious voyager to the 'Long Branch of the Pacific.' At the sound of that ringing and echoing neigh, the old stage horse assumed a slow and sombre gait, and the drivers drew up in a very meditative frame of mind. . . . All the rest of Santa Cruz stepped more briskly, and smiled more cheerfully, and everybody said to his neighbor, 'Now is the winter of our discontent made glorious summer.'"

So the connection was made. Iron and flesh horses now shared the rails, occasionally with dramatic results as reported by the *Sentinel:*

> "Last Saturday afternoon, a street car on the Chestnut street line came near being smashed to smithereens. The driver attempted to make an extra trip to carry away a number of persons from the bathhouses, and when near the Felton wharf he heard the whistle of the Santa Cruz train on its way to Watsonville. Both on the same track. The driver whipped his horse into a gallop and just as he entered the cut he was greeted with loud, sharp whistling and the train was nigh onto the horsecar. Luckily the train was stopped and the horsecar rolled onto the side track."

There were other incidents. Finally one episode drew a stern rebuke from the *Sentinel's* editor: "Last Sunday morning one of the streetcars on Chestnut Street, filled with men, women, and children, came near running into a train which was crossing the track at the lower end of the avenue. It is usual for the driver to let the horse trot along while he collects fare, and in this instance he was collecting fare and did not hear the locomotive whistle, and only observed what the matter was when he saw passengers attempting to jump from the car. It was by a miracle the car was not demolished and some of the passengers killed, as the cars passed each other there was hardly six inches of space between the two. Who is to blame for this piece of carelessness?"

These were just near-misses, raising blood pressures but no great public outcry. The horsecars continued to be well patronized, wending their way daily to the beach except during the stormiest of the winter months.

On January 12, 1877, Hihn legally separated his horsecar operations from the steam railroad and formalized them as the *City Railroad Company,* incorporated for 50 years with a capital stock of $10,000 ($2,000 subscribed, of which Hihn pledged $1,985). Five directors were named including four of German extraction: John Werner; jeweler William Effey; blacksmith and carriage-shopkeeper Edward Foster; and George Otto, proprietor of Otto's Hall and the Soquel Sugar Works. The fifth was bachelor and Dartmouth College graduate John Brazer, who had come to Santa Cruz in the 1860s to establish a bookshop and stationery store. The company's beachfront terminus was moved from the San Lorenzo east bank to the Leibbrandt bathhouse.

Hihn also proceeded to formalize his 1872 State Legislature horsecar franchise. The instrument in this case was the *Front Street Railroad Company,* incorporated August 31, 1877, with $10,000 in capital stock and a 50-year charter. The specified route was from the Leibbrandt bathhouse through private lands and Cliff Street up the west boundary of the San Lorenzo to Bridge Street, Front Street, and the Lower Plaza. Named directors were Hihn, Amasa Pray, and a trio of well-regarded Santa Cruzans: Franklin Cooper, Superintendent of Schools Hampton E. Makinney (late of Placerville), and Elihu Anthony, a 68-year-old Methodist minister-businessman with an impressive list of Santa Cruz "firsts": first postmaster, first chairman County Board of Supervisors, first subdivider, builder of the first local foundry (said to be only the third foundry built in California), and co-founder of Santa Cruz's first Protestant church. The company's secretary was attorney James O. Wanzer, secretary of the Racing Association and, like Anthony, a New York native. Each man pledged $1,000 to the Front Street company.

3. Triumph and Tribulation

THESE WERE days of triumph for Hihn and his colleagues, although tensions were mounting among the Santa Cruz Railroad's directors and in their relations with the town and county. The new steam railroad generated substantial lumber and passenger trade, reporting a $50,000 return over its first six months of full-scale operation. It also allowed Hihn to develop valuable redwood tracts back of Aptos and in the mountains between there and Watsonville. But it never carried the volume for which it was designed, and operations proved costly. Washouts were common; service was suspended for days on end. One train trapped by successive washouts took three days to cover the 20 miles from Santa Cruz to Watsonville.

Taxpayer suits had blocked delivery for more than a year of $114,000 in county subsidies pledged to the road. These were freed in February and March 1876, but when Hihn sought $7,800 more covering further construction, he was forced to go to court. The legislative act allowing county governments to fund railroad construction had been repealed in 1874; the supervisors now claimed they were not compelled (perhaps not even permitted) to honor previous agreements with the railroad. Hihn eventually won this suit but not before an eight-year legal battle finally resolved by the U.S. Supreme Court, which ordered the supervisors to pay the subsidy and accumulated interest for 5½ years at 7% per annum.

Pressed for funds, Hihn vainly made application to the Santa Cruz Common Council (it was now a city) to reduce its tax assessment from $5,000 to $3,000 per mile for right of way and from $650 to $470 per mile for rolling stock. He also went to court opposing a *post facto* $225 annual license fee imposed by the city. This battle he won but only after another long court fight.

Most damaging was a parting of the ways between Hihn and Spreckels, the latter refusing in mid-1878 to pay a $10-per-share assessment on capital stock of the Santa Cruz Railroad (Hihn owned 2,400 shares and Spreckels 1,605). Hihn took Spreckels to court in April 1879 asking $16,050 and back interest for a year. This case never came to a full accounting because Hihn stepped down in February 1881 as president of the Santa Cruz Railroad, arranging for its acquisition by the Southern Pacific. The transfer was made through a bankruptcy proceeding, the Southern Pacific taking full charge of the narrow gauge in April 1882 and standard-gauging it the following year.

PACIFIC AVENUE HORSECAR approaches Lower Plaza, late 1880s.

UCSC, Preston Sawyer Collection

4. Horsecar Competition

THE LITTLE red cars of the *City Railroad* continued to ply their trade up and down Chestnut Street. For two years the "red line" faced no competition. Waiting in the wings, however, were the "yellow line" cars of the *Pacific Avenue Street Railroad Company*, likewise fathered by a steam road, the Santa Cruz and Felton.

Although Hihn had first proposed the Santa Cruz-Felton logging railroad, it was other interests—a Santa Clara County syndicate—who laid down definitive plans in 1874 for a narrow-gauge pike down the San Lorenzo riverbank to the tideline in or near Santa Cruz. In the vanguard were ex-Australian Edmund J. Cox, grain dealer John S. Carter, attorney Charles Silent, and mill owner Cornelius G. Harrison, all of San Jose, plus several others. They filed for incorporation in November 1874 as *The Santa Cruz and Felton Rail Road Company.*

Behind this plan lay several hoped-for advantages. The Los Gatos wagon road used for hauling crossed the private lands of Isaac Graham, who collected a stiff fee on each load. The area's lumbermen wanted to bypass Graham's toll road. Also, in January 1874, the State Legislature had passed an act providing for construction of a 20-mile-long lumber flume from the headwaters of the San Lorenzo to the Pacific, with enough capability to perhaps double the area's output of cut lumber. Government funds were available. So the Santa Clara group secured these funds and organized the *San Lorenzo Flume*

and Lumber Company, substituting rail service for the flume below Felton.

Of special interest was that Silent and Harrison both were experienced horsecar promoters well aware that property values went up wherever horsecars ran. The German-born Silent had served as incorporator and secretary of the *San Jose and Santa Clara Railroad Company* (1868), the West's first interurban horsecar line. Harrison and others were even now negotiating to build the *North Side Horse Railroad* in San Jose, a potential challenger to the San Jose and Santa Clara.

Their influence was felt when, on January 9, 1875, the Santa Cruz town fathers gave the Santa Cruz and Felton a franchise through town allowing the company to assign all rights to a street railway if built. Permission was given to operate along River Street, Mission Street, and Pacific Avenue to a wharf "to be constructed by grantee at the foot of Pacific Avenue." Operation over most of the distance was limited to horsepower, and the company was required to fill and grade the east side of Pacific Avenue between Elm and Maple Streets. The company's ultimate intent—widely advertised—was to tunnel under Mission Hill from Mission Orchard (north River Street) and provide an altogether different route to the beach, leaving horsecars in charge of service down the avenue from the Lower Plaza to the beach.

This was confirmed January 13 when the city separately franchised Silent and associates to operate a horse railroad from Mission and Walnut Streets up Mission to the Lower Plaza, thence down Pacific Avenue through Mrs. Blackburn's lands to Bay Street and the tideline. Horsepower was stipulated, as was iron rail and macadam or plank surfacing between the rails, two feet on each side and the full street width at intersections. Provision was made for joint use of the rails by other companies up to 600 feet in length, on payment by those companies of half the cost and maintenance. Switches and turnouts were forbidden on Pacific Avenue from the Lower Plaza to Lincoln Street. The franchise specified operation from the corner of River and Mission Streets to the tideline within one year and over the entire distance by July 1, 1877.

The first date was met in October 1875 when the Santa Cruz and Felton ran its first train through Pacific Avenue to its new 1278-foot wharf—rebuilt from an 1855 pier and rechristened the "railroad wharf." That same month Santa Cruz granted rights for a 900-foot Mission Hill tunnel and route down Chestnut Street paralleling the Santa Cruz Railroad. This work was completed the following year, and the Santa Cruz and Felton commenced full-scale steam service down Chestnut Street to the wharf. Pacific Avenue was temporarily left untenanted.

On April 5, 1876, Silent and associates were franchised by the city to extend their proposed horsecar line from Bay Street and Pacific Avenue to the Leibbrandt bathhouse, again paralleling the Santa Cruz Railroad. The following October they incorporated the *Pacific Avenue Street Railroad Company* with Silent, Carter, and Harrison among the directors. Cox, by now an incorporator of the Santa Cruz County Bank of Savings and Loan, was named treasurer. Newcomers to the board were C.B. Gorrill of San Francisco; banker W.D. Tisdale of San Jose; Bernard Peyton, superintendent of the sprawling California Powder Works at nearby Powder Mill Flat; and James Pieronnet Pierce, New York emigrant who had amassed a small fortune in

JAMES P. PIERCE, lumberman, builder, and first owner of Pacific Avenue Street Railroad Company.
San Jose Public Library

California mining and turned his attention to other interests including manufacturing and banking. It was known that Pierce, who had recently moved from San Francisco to Santa Clara, planned to log the forests around Felton and Ben Lomond, where his investments were mounting. He had bought into the Santa Cruz and Felton and, with others, was projecting a network of narrow-gauge logging railroads above Felton. Pierce had resources sufficient if needed to challenge even those of Hihn.

PACIFIC AVENUE Street Railroad horsecar No. 3 passing Centennial Flour Mill on Beach Hill about 1878. The mill, built in 1876, burned in February 1904 together with two nearby planing mills. The intense heat cracked window glass in many Beach Hill residences.
UCSC, Preston Sawyer Collection

16

TINY OBJECT is a Pacific Avenue horsecar on the lower avenue, in the late 1880s. This view is from Beach Hill.

March 1877 brought news that Pierce had acquired controlling interest in the Pacific Avenue horsecar company, ordered cars for it, bought the necessary right of way from Mrs. Blackburn, and was grading near the Felton railroad beach cut. Hired to supervise the construction was Captain Richard W. Garratt, whose work building the Santa Cruz and Felton was well known. Reported the *Sentinel:* "The road will extend down Pacific Avenue to the foot-bridge at the base of the hill; thence to the right along the base of the hill through the lands of J.E. Butler and Allen & Co.; thence along the Felton Railroad to the warehouse of said Company; thence to the east of said warehouse. . . . In time the road will be continued up Mission Hill and down the beach." Service began incrementally as the line of construction passed the Centennial Mill and across the esplanade (now Beach Street) onto the railroad wharf. By midsummer the yellow cars of the Pacific Avenue line were a familiar sight on the avenue and the wharf, in competition with those of the "red line."

Both companies continued running well in January 1878 "doing a fair business," according to the *Sentinel.* But the onset of winter rains brought many problems especially to the "yellow line," which had not yet laid plank between its rails. Its horses, mired in the avenue mud, struggled valiantly to keep the cars rolling. "The streetcars run but semi-occasionally," reported the *Sentinel* in late February. "We have not seen them for several days on Pacific Avenue. Can't blame the companies for withdrawal of the cars, yet this is the time that people who have to travel to and from the beach need the cars most." That winter was particularly stormy, but a pattern was set whereby the horsecars tended to disappear during the winter rains and re-emerge only when the worst storms had passed.

PACIFIC AVENUE horsecar passing under Grand Arch N.S.G.W. on Pacific Avenue. View, probably taken in September 1888, is north from Cooper St. *UCSC, Preston Sawyer Collection*

5. The Opera House Episode

SANTA CRUZ'S population by 1878 had reached nearly 6,000 permanent inhabitants, with patronage enough for both horsecar companies. Competition settled to a measured pace. In April came announcement that the Pacific Avenue company would soon extend its rails to the Leibbrandt bathhouse as provided by its April 1876 franchise, but nothing happened. Both streetcar avenues—Pacific and Chestnut—remained unpaved and in disgraceful condition. Certain planked intersections in Pacific Avenue were said to be traps for the unwary; promised improvements were not forthcoming.

In September Hihn planked his railroad bridge over the San Lorenzo and inaugurated horsecar service to Wood's Lagoon whenever traffic warranted. But with the start of winter rains the "red line" went into hiding for about two months (until late February 1879).

October 1878 brought the first hint in the *Sentinel* that the directors of the Santa Cruz and Felton—now including Pierce—might sell the little logging road if the price and conditions were right. The obvious buyer would be the aggressive *South Pacific Coast* narrow gauge of Alfred (Hog) Davis and Senator James G. Fair, even now pressing southward from Oakland and San Jose across the mountains toward the Pacific in or near Santa Cruz. Negotiations continued for some months during which the South Pacific Coast essayed a route paralleling the Felton road down the far bank of the San Lorenzo. But June 1879 brought confirmation of a lease agreement whereby the South Pacific Coast took managerial control of the smaller company's tracks, rolling stock, and flume. Control passed to the South Pacific Coast on July 26 when Davis became president of the Felton road, Cox, Garratt, Carter, Harrison, Gorrill, and Pierce remaining as directors. Certain changes were necessary, including relaying the Felton ties with heavier rail. The first South Pacific Coast train rolled into Santa Cruz May 14, 1880, commencing direct service to San Jose, Oakland, and East Bay communities.

Sale of the Felton road to the Davis-Fair interests was a blow to Hihn's Santa Cruz Railroad and horsecar operations, although the new railroad brought him gain from another quarter. As the *Sentinel* observed: "Some men are born rich, others acquire riches, others have riches thrust upon them, and some are lucky. We think F.A. Hihn is the lucky man this time. When land was of little value in this county, he succeeded to the ownership of the Augmentation Rancho, a large portion of which, although heavily timbered, was mountainous and rough, and appeared to be next to valueless. Now, with the new railroad putting tunnels into the Santa Cruz Mountains, the timber must be purchased from Mr. Hihn. And when the tunnels are finished, the whole Santa Clara Valley will be his customer." However, direct service over the mountains pinched off Hihn's most lucrative market, Santa Cruz, diminishing both the income and the worth of his railroad proper-

ties. The sale also freed Pierce to devote more attention to affairs of his Pacific Avenue horsecar company, somewhat neglected during the past two years. This prospect must have been disheartening because Hihn, in addition to his legal battles with the city fathers and county supervisors, was now also jousting in the courts with Pierce, for whom he had little personal liking.

The issue in question seems petty today, but at the time it was a matter of burning community interest. It concerned ownership and control of the Opera House on Pacific Avenue, and it underscored the many personality differences between the two men. Both were financially successful, though by different means. Hihn, who knew failure, was characterized by loyalty (especially to his German friends). Affable, blunt, and determined to succeed, he was dedicated to a deep personal sense of ethics that brooked few compromises. It was characteristic of him, for instance, to use the courts continuously for redress of wrongs—to oppose a *post facto* licensing fee, to seek justice in a foreclosure hearing, contract dispute, or disagreement among partners. Principles rather than costs were often at stake. He considered legal responsibilities more inviolable perhaps than any other personal matters, and once remarked that he spent more time in courthouses than most lawyers and some judges.

Hihn's penchant for righteousness extended beyond the courtroom. He was George Otto's chief bondsman when the latter, as county treasurer, misappropriated county funds in 1879. As bondsman Hihn was responsible for the losses and made good the obligation after some astute wrangling to fix the exact loss. A year later he took over Otto's Soquel Sugar Works for $100 at a sheriff's sale and considered the scales balanced. So did the community; no one else bid.

Hihn was a shrewd businessman, feared in some quarters but generally respected, comfortable with the wealthy and politically powerful but also with section hands and horsecar drivers. His annual birthday parties in later years, after the turn of the century, were celebrations of local note, remarked by all segments of the community.

Pierce in many respects had followed an easier course: American in background, quite different in temperament. From his mining ventures he took $500,000 to San Francisco and more than that when he moved to Santa Clara. An accomplished financier, promoter, and builder, he became president of the Pacific Manufacturing Company and also the Bank of Santa Clara, a respected community leader and public benefactor admired by friends and peers. He expected admiration. He preferred perseverance and personal diplomacy to confrontation. Fully capable of altruistic sentiments, he was less concerned with small matters of principle than larger issues of purpose. He was quieter and more easygoing than Hihn.

Thus came Pierce to Santa Cruz, a community he admired, riding a wave of success. He expected to be well met and, at first, contemplated substantial investments. But confrontations with Hihn and others quelled his enthusiasm. He saw Hihn as irascible; Hihn considered Pierce a man of small moment. "He is not a wise man," Hihn would say, wagging his head. Eventually Pierce relocated in Alameda, where he died in 1897 still professing bitterness toward Santa Cruz.

The Opera House episode dramatized the Hihn-Pierce antipathy. In 1877 a promoter named Budd Smith—a man of imagination but little means—won local support for a theater to serve the community, with himself as manager. Hihn gave land and Pierce donated lumber from his Ben Lomond mill and transported it free of charge. The theater was built, but no sooner had it opened than Smith ran out of money. Pierce stepped in to run the Opera House.

Hihn took umbrage with these goings-on, which in his opinion brought Pierce to ownership of property for which the latter had not paid. Hihn's gift deed was ironclad and the property was not recoverable, but close scrutiny showed that the deed did not cover a narrow, inches-wide strip fronting on Pacific Avenue. That strip was legally Hihn's. So he went to court seeking recovery or recompense.

The courts finally found for Pierce, but the episode left bad feelings between the men that were never resolved.

6. Demise of the 'Red Line'

FREED FROM his Felton railroad commitments, Pierce indeed turned his attention to horsecar matters. Christian Hoffman, local realtor and a director of the Bank of Santa Cruz, became superintendent of the Pacific Avenue company. Rolling stock was refurbished and new cars added, including "an open palace car that cost in San Francisco $606. It is all the rage among travelers," reported the *Sentinel*; "a second one, not quite so heavy, will be built here."

In November 1879 the company reduced its fares to 5¢ per ride, 25 tickets to the dollar.

The long-awaited extension of the "yellow line" along the beach also materialized. On August 2, 1879, Pierce affirmed his earlier plans and, the following week, petitioned the Common Council not only for the beachfront extension but also for confirmation of his company's franchise up Mission Hill and out Mission Street. The company needed this, he explained, before going to the expense of extending the road to the bathhouses.

The council deferred its decision, then responded September 15 by ordering both streetcar companies and both railroads—the Felton and the Santa Cruz—to plank between their rails on heavily traveled streets as required by their franchises. Pierce's reply must have been affirmative. On September 22 the council gave him two franchises: one from Mission Street and Walnut Avenue via Mission, Pacific, and the beach-front—north of the Santa Cruz Railroad—to the San Lorenzo River, and the other from Pacific Avenue through the lands of Isaac L. Thurber to the river, then southeasterly along its west bank to strike the first line. The latter to some extent duplicated Hihn's 1872 State Legislature franchise.

Construction of the beachfront extension got under way almost at once. "The work is substantial," noted the *Sentinel* on November 8. "Where a foundation of earth is used, the sand is removed to bedrock and the space filled with broken rock. To make room for Liddell's bathhouses (west of Leibbrandt's), the rear bank is being excavated in for a distance of 40 feet. Piles will be used for the road here and beyond."

By January 3, 1880, work was nearly done to the Leibbrandt bathhouses, which were set back slightly to accommodate the horsecar tracks. Construction stopped briefly to fix the right of way across the Leibbrandt property bordering the steam railroad. On January 25, cars of the Pacific Avenue company rolled to their new terminus near the river mouth. The company reported expenses of $5,000. "They are determined to be a first-class road," declared the *Sentinel*.

"Yellow line" service was suspended briefly in March to allow for filling and changing the grade on Pacific Avenue. The line was also extended up Mission Hill to Pope House, fulfilling in part the franchise obligation to run rails to Mission and Walnut. Twenty-minute headway was established to and from the beach, with service from 8 A.M. to 9:20 P.M. (to the river mouth only when patronized and not up Mission Hill after 6 P.M.). In August the Common Council gave Pierce a one-year extension to comply fully with both franchises.

The "red line," meanwhile, suffered declining fortunes. Although reluctant, Hihn complied in November 1879 with the council's edict to plank between his rails in Chestnut Street. Filling and surfacing that street caused a suspension of "red line" service that lasted well into the following spring. The *Sentinel* reported both lines back in service in early May 1880 and doing a good business, considering the season.

"Red line" service was again suspended the following winter, this time permanently. By mid-February 1881 Hihn had laid off all railroad employees except for a clerk closing the books and 13 men repairing a wrecked bridge. His sale of the Santa Cruz Railroad and City Railroad to the Southern Pacific was announced locally on April 28.

Further action was delayed almost a year. In March 1882 the Southern Pacific, readying to complete its acquisition of the Santa Cruz Railroad, petitioned the Common Council in behalf of the railroad to abandon

By The Sea,

AS BEACHGOERS STROLL along the boardwalk, Pacific Avenue horsecars Nos. 2 and 5 run westbound on the Esplanade, where Beach St. is today. Note the standard-gauge steam railroad track behind the cars.
Randolph Brandt Collection

By The Sea,

AWAITING PATRONS, Pacific Avenue horsecar No. 5 stops at Neptune Baths on the beach, late 1880s. Note row of decorative palms shown more fully grown in later photographs. *UCSC, Preston Sawyer Collection*

By The Beautiful Sea!

SEA BEACH HOTEL (large structure behind building at left) opened in 1888. Pacific Avenue horsecar No. 7 heads eastbound toward beachfront terminus. Freight car on wharf at right is on narrow-gauge South Pacific Coast Railroad, sold in 1887 to Southern Pacific.
UCSC, Preston Sawyer Collection

the horsecar franchise and remove the tracks from Mission, Vine, Cherry, and Rincon streets. These rights were granted April 3 after the Southern Pacific changed its petition to read "City Railroad Company" instead of "Santa Cruz Railroad." The rails were removed. No record has been found of the final disposition of either the rails or the horsecars.

There remained only one more item of "red line"

business and that, a technicality. On July 26, in San Francisco, the Southern Pacific named a new board of directors for the City Railroad Company; George Crocker became president. This action did not have to be repeated. The company disappeared as a legal entity, swallowed up in one of the burgeoning mergers that characterized the corporate growth of the Southern Pacific.

7. The Midnight Switch

WITH HIHN gone as a competitor, Pierce reincorporated the *Pacific Avenue Street Railroad Company* on March 9, 1882, for a term of 50 years and a capital stock of $100,000. Named to the new board were Cox, Captain Garratt, Hoffman, Pierce, and his son Richard T. Pierce of Santa Clara, then a young man. Hoffman became company treasurer as well as superintendent. Ownership was vested 7/10 in James Pierce, 2/10 in Hoffman, and 1/10 in Garratt. The company charter specified service from Mission and Locust Streets through the Lower Plaza to the beach and thence to the mouth of the San Lorenzo. No mention was made of the secondary route down the riverbank, this route apparently having been abandoned.

In May the Common Council again franchised the company for 50 years to operate from Mission and Walnut to the beach, service to commence over the entire route within one year. This time the charter wiped out previous restrictions on a switch in Pacific Avenue between the Lower Plaza and Lincoln Street, Pierce arguing persuasively that a doubling of "yellow line" service—desired by all parties—required such a switch. It was this action which, a few months later, was to stir up a fiery local controversy.

Patrons were generally satisfied with the service and looked forward to increased frequency. Yet, as the company made ready to install the switch, tempers flared. Certain property owners, among them Hihn and his brother Hugo, a Mr. Holbrook, and Duncan McPherson, owner of the Duncan Block and publisher of the *Sentinel*, bitterly opposed the switch, which was laid in front of the Duncan Block. McPherson took the company to court demanding its removal. On December 16, the company capitulated, took out the switch, and paid court costs of $13.55. Ruffled by the proceedings, however, the company then went back to the Common Council and got, on January 15, 1883, specific permission to locate its switch on the east side of Pacific near Lincoln.

Pierce later told friends that he tried, unsuccessfully, to reason with McPherson, meeting the editor on the porch of the Duncan Block for a conversation that was locally notorious but never reported. From that time on, it was said, Pierce cherished a contempt for McPherson that he never lost opportunity to express. Meanwhile, using the *Sentinel's* editorial columns, McPherson flailed away at Pierce on a variety of

counts. The Pacific Avenue company, he wrote, had claimed "improvement" of the avenue, yet owned only an uncleaned stable with piles of manure and an unwhitewashed carbarn. The track was in disgraceful condition. The railroad, he said, had tried to abandon Mission Street and now ran as few cars as compelled to. It had not complied with conditions of its franchise, which should now be revoked. "I thought we were free from all the troubles with these railroads," McPherson stormed.

Hihn took more direct action. On learning that the horsecar tracks were entirely on his side of Pacific Avenue (facing his property and that of his brother Hugo), he laid asphaltum snug up to the nearest rail, thus preventing Pierce and Hoffman from installing the switch short of ripping out the new pavement.

It was in this climate, on February 5, that the Common Council met to reconsider the switch matter. Hihn rose to brand it a nuisance—a ridiculous spectacle, jeered the *Sentinel,* for one who himself had been a "collector of 5¢ fares." Another fierce debate arose in council chambers a week later, at which time Pierce agreed henceforth to have his horsecars built locally. (This had been another prong of the *Sentinel's* attack.) Nonetheless the councilmen backed down, now claiming that they intended only for the sidetrack (switch) to be located below Laurel Street.

McPherson was mollified and, when Pierce ordered three cars from local builder Evan Lukens and five loads of gravel to relay track in the Lower Plaza, the *Sentinel's* tone became conciliatory. "The street railway is doing a good job of moving its track into the center of the roadbed at Briody's Corner," it reported. Certain property owners were found, among them John Werner and William Effey, who were willing to have the switch in front of their stores. The Common Council passed a bill, enacted early in March, allowing the company switches west of Leibbrandt's and in the avenue south of Lincoln, which Hoffman opined would be adequate for five-minute headway if found profitable. The new switch in the avenue would be covered with asphaltum (not left open).

Peace had seemingly descended but one last flurry remained, described at length by the *Sentinel* on April 28 in an article entitled "Midnight Switching." Early the previous Sunday morning (April 22), shortly after midnight, there appeared on Pacific Avenue a gang from the South Pacific Coast Railroad, working for the street-car company, who began tearing up the macadam in front of the Holbrook residence preparing to lay the switch. A near fight ensued, but Mr. Holbrook could not reach his taller antagonist, presumably the crew boss. McPherson was roused between 1 and 2 A.M. but thought the message to be a prank, not realizing the full import until well into the morning. Hoffman, when contacted by McPherson, explained that early Sunday was the best time to do the job, when the South Pacific Coast crew was available. The work proceeded all day and the switch was in place by nightfall—"an exceedingly short switch," observed the *Sentinel*.

8. Laubens and Other Matters

BY NOW horsecars had established their place in the community, bringing their own special comedies and concerns. One late June night, for instance, a local businessman responded to a racket in the horsecar stables, discovering two stallions, loose, trying to chew up a third, fastened. At considerable risk he rescued the wounded horse, which was found to be badly bitten.

The following episode was recorded by the *Sentinel* in July 1884:

"Upon the back seat of a car otherwise crowded to the utmost, last evening, was space just large enough for one. From the steps on one side hastened a stout lady with a small boy, while from the other an ethereal young lady sprang lightly in, each hoping to win the vacant seat. The stout lady had rather the best of it, and she and her small boy managed to occupy the empty space in an exceedingly short space of time, but the young lady, not to be baffled, planted herself half upon the occupant's lap . . . and half upon the knee of the gentleman next to her. Neither had as yet barked at each other, but the youth, feeling herself defrauded, pressed her ethereal form on the two laps with force and emphasis, while the s. l. started to probe the y. l.'s back and sides with her elbows. Young lady remarked to her escort, loudly enough to be heard, 'This *person* thinks she is going to drive me out of this seat, but I'm going to sit right here all the way up.' At that time they looked at one another for the first time and discovered they were intimate acquaintances. The apologies and laughter that followed . . . were better than described."

Scarcely two months later came the following: "As one of the streetcars was departing the beach yesterday, a passenger boarded the car having in his possession a small box that excited the curiosity of a fellow passenger.

"Got a squirrel there?" said he.

"No, sir, nary a squirrel."

"Is it a seagull?"

"Nary seagull."

"Well, then, will you be so kind as to tell me what you have in that box."

"Certainly; there's no secret about it—it's a lauben."

"Now that's an animal I never heard of before. What's a lauben?"

"A lauben is—well, you know when a man has the 'jim-jams' he sees snakes, lizards, and all sorts of things, and a lauben is an animal that lives on these things."

"Well, that is funny," said the inquirer, and subsided by a moment, apparently satisfied by the explanation. Suddenly a thought seemed to strike him. "But," said he, "the snakes and lizards that a man sees when he has the 'jim-jams' are not real."

"That's where you are right," remarked the other, unabashed, as he stepped from the car which had now reached the Wilkins House, "and this isn't a real lauben."

One untended car trotted home to the carbarn on a summer's day of 1884, to the consternation of driver and passengers. But not all the incidents were funny. Horsecars sometimes ran amuck when the steeds were frightened. And the rails themselves, often above street grade, caused many accidents like the following: "A double team and carriage belonging to the City Stable containing a full load of pleasure seekers among which was a large sprinkling of ladies was being driven down Pacific Avenue at a good lively pace yesterday afternoon about one o'clock. When attempting to cross the railroad track in front of Williamson & Garrett's to turn into Walnut Avenue, one of the front wheels of the carriage caught in the flange of the track and tore it clear from the hub. Through the good managing of one that held the reins the team was immediately brought to a standstill, therefore causing no further harm more than very much frightening the lady occupants, who needed no second invitation to alight. That no one was killed or badly injured was no fault of the street car track." Efforts were made periodically to compel flat rail and conformance of horsecar grades with those of the city streets, but the problem persisted so long as horsecars clopped through the community.

9. Pierce Sells 'Yellow Line'

PIERCE WAS disenchanted and, although service was upgraded by the horsecar company, no substantial improvements could be expected. The company's rails to the river were removed during standard-gauging of the Santa Cruz Railroad in 1883. There was talk of rebuilding, but no action. About midyear 1883, service was halted up Mission Hill. Shortly after Christmas the company began paving over the tracks, as authorized in December by the Common Council. Pierce and associates were commended early in 1884 by the *Santa Cruz Surf* (rival of the *Sentinel*) for adding cars and switches at a cost of about $4,000 to double the service, but a storm of protest arose in April when they sought formal abandonment of all portions on Mission Street. The Common Council on April 7 approved the abandonment but then, on May 5, heard complaints from 14 influential property owners. Spokesman for the group was Felix Gambert, proprietor of Pope House and former manager of San Jose's Market Street and Willow

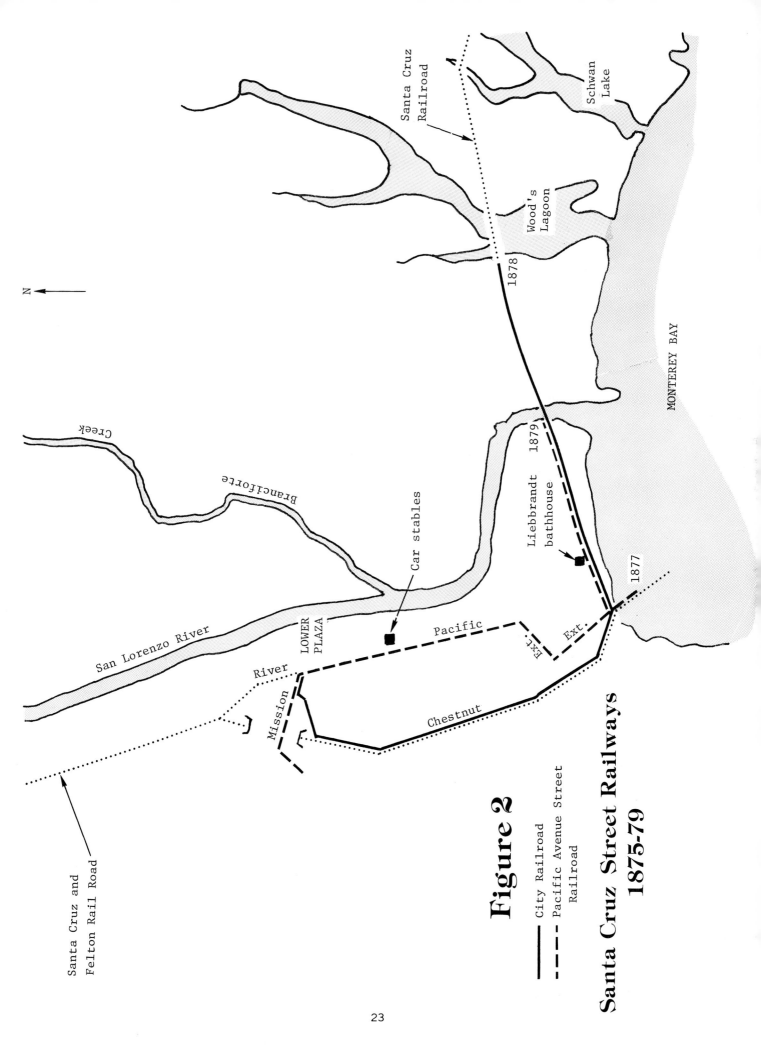

Figure 2

Santa Cruz Street Railways
1875-79

—— City Railroad
- - - Pacific Avenue Street Railroad

Santa Cruz Railroad

Schwan Lake

Wood's Lagoon

1878

MONTEREY BAY

N

Creek

Branciforte

Car stables

San Lorenzo River

LOWER PLAZA

Liebbrandt bathhouse

1879

Pacific

River

Mission

Ext.

Ext.

Ext.

1877

Chestnut

Santa Cruz and
Felton Rail Road

23

Glen horse railroad, who demanded that the Pacific Avenue company run cars on the hill and repair its switches under threat of forfeiting its charter. The council reversed its decision and ordered service restored; the company complied.

Pierce essentially withdrew from the road's management at this time, entrusting its fortunes to Christian Hoffman. Word passed that the company could be bought although there were no immediate takers, business being slow. The company's stock was pledged to secure loans from San Jose banking interests and administered by C.T. Ryland of that community.

A non-horsecar competitor emerged briefly in 1884: Lincoln and Hurbert's omnibus line operating half-hourly service down Mission Hill to the beach and charging a nickel fare. "The five-cent 'bus seems to catch the bulk of the patronage," observed the *Surf* in June. By September both lines were said to be busy both day and evening. The competition maintained for another year or so, but the omnibuses eventually disappeared.

Pierce found a buyer in 1887. The first hint came April 18 with Hoffman's resignation as superintendent of the road. This was followed April 29 by a business meeting from which the stockholders emerged "far from cool." The *Surf* reported a "reliable rumor" that the company would not make any daily deposits for a time and that Hoffman's resignation would lie on the table for an indefinite period.

Formal announcement of the sale came May 19. "Yesterday evening Messrs. E.J. Swift, Thomas Cole and Christian Hoffman returned from San Jose where they were on business relative to the transfer of the principal part of the stock of the *Pacific Avenue Street Railroad*. Messrs. Swift and Cole purchased the stock of the Hon. C.T. Ryland of San Jose and Mr. C. Hoffman of this place. The transfer was made yesterday in San Jose. Messrs. Swift and Cole, by this purchase, hold three-quarters of the stock of the road. Mr. Swift will probably be the superintendent of the line.

"It is the intention of the purchasers to give the public a better accommodation than has heretofore been given," continued the announcement. "More cars will be put on and the general facilities of the road will be greatly increased. The cars will run on quicker times than previously. In fact the new administration intend to increase the popularity of the road by giving the traveling public every advantage that can possibly be made. Mr. Cole is a gentleman of wealth who has lately come to this town, and who sees the chances for many profitable investments, and is a gentleman of a class greatly needed in Santa Cruz."

It was an admirable association. Cole, a native New Yorker in his late forties, was familiar with the community, having spent several summers in Santa Cruz. His wealth came from real estate and mining. He was an able administrator—former president of the Bullion and Chollar mining companies—and he enjoyed the day-by-day operations of the horsecar line. Elias J. Swift, then in his late thirties and also a native New Yorker,

was the visionary—a man who had traveled to California seeking adventure and fallen almost by happenstance into hotel management, taking over the Abbott House in Salinas in 1878. He had come to Santa Cruz in 1884 to assume management of the Pacific Ocean House for F.A. Hihn and recently, with Hihn, had leased Pope House, succeeding Felix Gambert. Swift was also negotiating to buy Kittridge House, another quality resort. He envisioned a master plan for Santa Cruz transit with a central beachfront train depot and network of local lines—probably electric streetcars—radiating in all directions to stimulate the community's growth.

There was a third, silent partner in the enterprise: veteran lawyer Charles B. Younger, longtime associate of Hihn in matters of railroad litigation and a former board member of the Santa Cruz Railroad. (Younger's son, Charles B. Jr., married Hihn's daughter and confidante, Agnes, in 1902.) Younger saw himself as responsible for the practical circumstances of the Pacific Avenue company: financing, franchise matters, etc. "The visionaries are the ones who bring me my business and also my headaches," he declared.

The company considered plans for electrifying the "yellow line" but deemed these premature. In a more practical vein, the horsecars were refurbished, repainted, and, according to the *Surf*, put in first-class condition. "New wheels and running gears have been put on each car. This renovating of the cars, the thorough repairing of the roadbed, the many new horses purchased and the increased number of cars running will afford more and better facilities for travel than ever before."

On April 28, 1888, Swift appeared before the Common Council asking franchise rights to extend the road up Mission Street to Fair Avenue (near the old racetrack) and build a branch from Pacific Avenue along the Laurel Street extension and Riverside Avenue to the beach. The latter was in essence a renewal of the company's 1879 franchise long abandoned. The requests were partly tactical in that a second group headed by capitalists John R. Chace and D. Younglove was now seeking a horsecar franchise from Pope House out Mission to Natural Bridges Park, with a branch down Walnut and Pacific Avenues to the Lower Plaza. Allied with this group was William Ely, who was soon to play a prominent role in developing East Santa Cruz transit. Younglove, a former associate of the Sacramento Electric Light Company, envisioned development of the ocean bluffs and lands out Mission Street. Subscriptions were sought from property owners along the route.

The idea elicited widespread support including an offer from Hihn to take $1,500 of stock and pay two-thirds of the cost for cutting down Weeks' Hill in Walnut Avenue. Commented the *Surf*: "Santa Cruz has arrived at the point now where the next principal movement in property and consequent enhancement of values will be in the direction which is characterized by enterprise and improvement. If property owners along the line of Mission Street will widen that thoroughfare and interest themselves to a proper extent in the street railroad enterprise, then we shall see the region from Bay View to the Moore ranch transformed from rural to suburban property and its intrinsic value nearly doubled."

Formal application was made by Chace and Young-love on April 2, 1888, and a preliminary ordinance was read by the Common Council eight days later. However, final approval stalled over matters of rail and gauge. The *Sentinel* advocated flat rail and standard gauge. The *Surf* predictably favored T rail and narrrow gauge, arguing that the stringers under flat bands would soon rot because of standing water and that standard gauge was too broad for Mission Street and Pacific Avenue. On May 16 the council's ordinance committee reported adversely on the Chace-Younglove application, having by then endorsed that of the Pacific Avenue company. Exclusive rights to Mission Street, plus the Laurel-Riverside branch, went to Cole, Swift, and associates.

The Pacific Avenue company introduced two-horse tandems in June 1888 to draw its cars up Mission Hill.

Swift's death on February 1, 1889, was a blow to his colleagues. He was then just 41 and a driving force in the company. To his estate passed 375 shares of stock valued at $15,000 but hypothecated to be worth only about $10,000 at his death. Kittridge House was sold. Swift's place as manager of the Pacific Ocean House and Pope House was taken by Edmund S. West, also a native New Yorker and former wharf manager for 15

years (1865-80) for the California Powder Works. West was a veteran dairyman, rancher, and employment consultant whose experience also included a brief stint in 1883 as railroad construction superintendent for the Southern Pacific in Monterey. He was soon named superintendent of the "yellow line."

Cole, who had previously mortgaged the road, declared his intent in September 1889 to press forward with an extension out Mission Street to Bay Street, to serve the new Garfield Park tabernacle being erected nearby on lands donated by Hihn, Abraham King of San Jose, and others to the Northern California Conference of Christian Churches. Plans called for a $14,000 octagonal structure surrounded by privately owned cottages and tenting grounds on bluffs overlooking the Pacific. The tabernacle was dedicated in September 1890, but the railroad extension failed to materialize.

There was another attempt late in 1889 by Chace and associates—now joined by E.H. Robinson, a prominent local realtor and merchant—to secure a franchise out Mission Street from the city center to Garfield Park. This bid also came to naught. What had captured the community's fancy in the meantime was an ambitious plan, rumored for more than a year, to build a new horsecar line from the city to East Santa Cruz and Twin Lakes, opening these areas for development. The architect of this scheme was William Ely, a respected local capitalist, bank director, property owner, and community leader.

POPE HOUSE, famous Mission Hill Resort.   *Randolph Brandt Collection*

EAST SANTA CRUZ horsecar No. 2 in Soquel Road. Atop carbarn, at far left, was a weathervane shaped like a horsecar.

Randolph Brandt Collection

10. East Santa Cruz Horse Railroad

DURING THE past year, suburban East Santa Cruz had experienced phenomenal growth: 100 buildings erected in less than 12 months. Plans were under way for Baptist conference grounds at Twin Lakes similar to those at Garfield Park. Sentiment in the suburb ran strong for better roads and facilities including horsecar service. That residents were willing to help pay for the improvements was evidenced at a public meeting in September 1889 at Lodtman's Hall in East Santa Cruz, to raise support and funds for better roads.

After several meetings with local citizens, Ely approached the county supervisors November 4 for a horsecar franchise up Soquel Road (now Soquel Avenue) from the Santa Cruz east city limits (Ocean Street) to Arana Gulch, a distance of about two miles. This franchise was granted December 3. He had meanwhile petitioned the Santa Cruz Common Council for rights to a street railway from the Lower Plaza—Front and Cooper Streets—along Front to Minnesota Avenue (also now Soquel Avenue), thence across a new private

bridge just north of the existing covered bridge and out Minnesota to the city limits. The council gave permission December 10, specifying flat rail, standard gauge, a nickel fare, and an obligation to run cars daily over the entire length of the road to maintain the franchise. This ordinance gave Ely a choice of motive power: horses, mules, electric motors, or wire rope (cable) running under the railroad.

Ely accepted these provisions and, on December 12, incorporated his new venture as the *East Santa Cruz Street Railroad Company*, with a capital stock of $20,000 and subscription of $5,000 pledged equally by five incorporators: Ely, Oliver H. Bliss, quarry operator Isaac L. Thurber, former tavern owner and Azores emigrant Jackson Sylvar, and bank cashier William D. Haslam, a Santa Cruz native and son of a former city clerk. Ely said some limited public subscription would be accepted and announced he was ready if need be to invest $25,000 in the enterprise. At a stockholders' meeting December 28, the incorporators were confirmed as directors of the company, Ely becoming president and general manager with Thurber vice president, Sylvar treasurer, and Haslam secretary. Work would commence, Ely declared, as soon as the winter weather settled.

The building of this new road would require solutions to many problems such as the new bridge, acceptable track grades, and the leveling of a formidable hill in Soquel Road. Also to be resolved were matters of rail and gauge. Despite the franchise conditions, Ely favored T rail and narrow gauge. The franchise would have to be altered, and that would demand tact.

Ely considered himself equal to the task, a man equipped by temperament, experience, and 20 years of community associations to handle the technical and political complexities. Born 1828 in New York State, he had migrated first to Illinois, where he worked in a woolen mill, and then in 1850 to California, where he tried mining. Discouraged, he turned to potato farming (a failure in 1852) and then to cattle, in which he prospered. Moving to Santa Cruz in 1869, he invested heavily in real estate and continued ranching and farming, becoming known locally as "a practical man and heavy taxpayer." In 1877, with Christian Hoffman and others, he was named a director of the Bank of Santa Cruz County, serving that institution for many years. Ely had many friends and associates in Santa Cruz to whom he could look for support.

Appointing himself construction superintendent, he attacked the problems with gusto, ordering equipment and materials and letting the necessary contracts. To Cunningham and Company went the award for ties, stringers, and bridge lumber totaling some 125,000 board feet plus 50 pilings, after demurs by several other companies because of the short March 30 delivery date. To Evan Lukens, the Park Street blacksmith and car-builder went the contract for cars. On February 22 Ely reached accord with the San Francisco Bridge Company on terms for the San Lorenzo bridge: $5,207 total, comprising $3,762.50 for four spans and five piers, plus 321 feet of trestle at $4.50 per linear foot. The new structure would require moving the footwalk from the north to the south side of the old bridge. Meanwhile, construction was proceeding on the company's new stables and car shop in the Soquel Road-Doyle Street triangle near Netherton and Williams' grocery. This work was finished early in March.

Two carloads of 48-pound T rail arrived February 9 from San Francisco, signaling Ely's intent to use these rather than flat rail. He again approached the Santa Cruz Common Council, securing on March 3 an amended franchise that allowed T rail and a 3'6" gauge. This ired the *Surf*. "What does it mean?" it asked plaintively.

"'Standard gauge' when applied to railroads is properly supposed to mean four feet eight inches in width, a width which, according to the wording of the franchise, would 'permit vehicles to travel over and across the same without trouble or inconvenience.' Either the ordinance granting the franchise means something or it doesn't," complained the *Surf*. "If the

FANCY WOOD-FRAME STORES faced on a graded earth street in East Santa Cruz, in the early 1890s. William Ely began running horsecars to this suburban community in May 1890.
Randolph Brandt Collection

franchise authorizes the construction of a street railway without regard to width, then the people must hereafter 'hold the peace.'

"This is not a matter of today, it is for all time. Every person of insight into futurity can see that this road is bound for Capitola; that it holds the key to the situation for a traffic which in twenty years from now will be large and lucrative. This is a question of right, and a matter of principle is involved. The merits or advantages of a narrow or a broad gauge are not under consideration, but simply the rights acquired under the franchises granted this road, and the representations upon which they were obtained. Now is the time when this matter should be attended to."

Despite these protests, construction began March 10 on the bridge and the following day on the line itself with the laying of a switch—T rail, 3'6" gauge—from the stables into Soquel Road. Within a few days Ely had several teams and 22 men at work. The crown of the Soquel Road hill was cut back to bedrock and the surplus earth used to fill a hollow at the base of the hill.

By March 29 track had been laid from Cayuga Street to west of Ocean Street. The *Surf* commended Ely and colleagues for a first-class job. "The grade is better than many supposed possible for an exit from the city to the east. On the bridge, the street railway extension is nine feet wide, leaving two and a half feet in the clear for foot passengers between the siding of the bridge and a passing car on the railway. On the outer side of the track, four turnouts will be built and provided with seats so that pedestrians can wait the arrival or the passage of a car at their convenience. The track layers today will reach the present terminus of the road at Cooper Street, and two more days should carry them to the Lower Plaza."

By April 5 the track laying was finished except on the bridge, whose construction was being pushed. By late April the work was so nearly done that Ely chose May Day (May 1) for the official opening. All Santa Cruz prepared for the celebration and especially East Santa Cruz, whose merchants hung red, white, and blue bunting.

It was a gala day. Three of Lukens' cars were in service: one closed, two open. Free rides were offered.

The three cars, said the *Surf*, were crowded for the most part all day. "The 'opening day' of the road was a success, and the promoters were radiant in their happiness at the smooth working of the road. The cars will be run daily, but no regular schedule will be put into practice until Monday (May 5). The schedule will be made so as to accommodate people engaged in business or at work in this city who live in East Santa Cruz, especially in regard to leaving East Santa Cruz in the morning and returning home in the evening."

Regular service began as planned. Horsecars of the East Santa Cruz railroad were soon a familiar sight along Soquel Road and crossing the river, with a 5¢ fare from the Lower Plaza to Cayuga Street, with drivers George Ely, John Soper, and Ed Ely at the reins. By mid-May the company was reporting more business than expected: about 400 passengers on Sundays and 200 on other days. It was already meeting expenses, said the directors, much sooner than anticipated.

RAILROAD AVENUE (now Seabright Avenue) in the late 1880s. William Ely chose this avenue and Cayuga Street for extending his East Santa Cruz horsecar line to Twin Lakes in September 1890. *Randolph Brandt Collection*

11. Twin Lakes and Arana Gulch

ON MARCH 3 Ely and his colleagues had petitioned the county supervisors for a branch line from Soquel Road out Cayuga Street to its end, a distance of about 2,100 feet. Commented the *Surf*: "Cayuga Street, if extended toward the bay to the Southern Pacific railroad track, would pass through the lands of Mrs. Vincent and daughter, and negotiations are pending to have the street opened. It can hardly be possible that the street will not be opened as a streetcar line running by all the adjacent property would at least double in value, and then the streetcar line would be continued about to Seabright Beach. The petition states that, if the franchise is granted, a flat railroad will be built, with three feet and six inches between the rails, and that at least one trip per hour will be made from sunrise to sunset daily, and as much oftener as business will justify, and that the road is to be completed before May 1, 1891."

The supervisors were not quick to respond because, successes notwithstanding, there were problems with the Ely Road yet to be resolved. For example, the replacement sidewalk on the covered bridge was narrower and considered inferior to its predecessor. An estimated $1,000 was needed to restore Soquel Road to its preconstruction condition. The track grade was higher than the street grade in this road (the Common Council had considered a similar problem in Front Street and decided, lacking leverage, that the best they could do was declare the elevated grade a nuisance). Finally there was the matter of priorities. If the new franchise were awarded, would Ely guarantee to complete the Arana Gulch extension?

Ely appeared before the board on May 10 promising to lower the track grade or raise the entire road as directed by the supervisors, at company expense. This he would do, he told them, even though he had already put five times as much earth on each side of the track as required by his contract. He also agreed to start work on the Arana Gulch extension by June 10 or 15. Thus assured, the supervisors gave him rights down Cayuga Street, Pilkington Lane or an alternate, and Railroad Avenue (now Seabright Avenue) to Atlantic Avenue, thence easterly down the hill to Wood's Lagoon, across a new bridge, and out East Cliff Drive to Central Avenue. This branch would serve the beaches and Twin Lakes conference grounds of the Baptist Resort Association. The company's articles of incorporation were amended June 3 to add the new line (total length all routes now to be 3½ miles) and to increase the capital from $20,000 to $70,000 with $13,500 subscribed: Ely $4,500, Bliss $4,000, Sylvar $2,500, Thurber and Haslam $1,000 each, and newspaperman William T. Vahlberg $500.

Some materials for the Twin Lakes branch were on the ground in late June, but the work was delayed until August 1. Ely later described this branch—more than a mile in length—as the crookedest piece of streetcar road in California. The rails had to be specially made to a fit of $\frac{1}{16}$ inch. Ely claimed that when he presented his diagram at the rolling mills, they asked him if he was trying to run the railroad into every man's dooryard.

Despite all, the line was operating by September 1, providing 5¢ service from the Lower Plaza to Twin Lakes.

"All for a nickel!" proclaimed the *Surf* on September 13. "An enjoyable trip to take—the streetcar of the East Santa Cruz railway at the Plaza, at Cooper Street or at the bridge, and roll along over the bridge, past the pretty homes of Minnesota Avenue, up the hill and past numerous late improvements to Cayuga Street, thence, by way of Cayuga Street, across to Railroad Avenue and so to Seabright where that lively little suburb furnishes many good patrons to the new car line; so on along the cliff and across the bridge to Twin Lakes.

"Many people who have not visited Twin Lakes will do so now that the car line is finished and they will be astonished to find the changes and progress which have taken place in that district. The well-graded streets, the dozen cottages completed and underway, the neat little hotel, the wings, croquet and tennis grounds, bathing tents, boats and other means of enjoyment, the numerous tents for camping, the many swimmers in the surf and in the smoother water of the lake all make the scene a pleasant one. Numerous grown people and children have learned to swim very rapidly in the lake where the evaporation leaves the water salt and buoyant.

"The completion of the street railway will be a grand factor in Twin Lakes' advancement and will give our citizens another delightful chance for a half day's outing.

"To date 60 lots of Twin Lakes have been sold and some late payments have sufficed to cancel the entire cost of the improvements so far made. Twin Lakes has fair prospects for the future."

True to his word, Ely completed the stub line out Soquel Road to the hill above Arana Gulch. The county supervisors invested a sizable sum in 1890-91 to fill, grade, and improve the road through the gulch, and there was talk of extending the railroad to Soquel. However, this did not come about.

The company installed benches for patrons along the line and built small stations—"waiting rooms," the *Surf* called them—at three locations: Wood's Lagoon, the corner of Soquel and Cayuga, and in the Plaza at one corner of the "Fair property." In December 1890 Ely added a classy touch, providing the horses with bells. "This will notify waiting passengers of the car's approach," advised the *Surf*, "and keep them from getting discouraged."

UNUSUAL VIEW of East Santa Cruz horsecar on Atlantic Avenue shows Wood's Lagoon and area now known as Yacht Harbor.
UCSC, Preston Sawyer Collection

12. Demise of the 'Yellow Line'

COLE AND HIS Pacific Avenue partners were now battling serious community pressures to wrest away their Mission Street franchise if the promised extension was not built. In April 1890 they put men and teams to work installing culverts and generally improving the existing roadbed, requiring suspension once more of "yellow line" service up Mission Hill. This annoyed both newspapers; the work was quickly finished and service restored up the hill.

Also in April the company, at its annual meeting, affirmed Cole as president and West as superintendent. Cole, West, and Younger were reelected to the board. Joining them as directors were T.V. Mathews and also John R. Chace, leader of the 1888 opposition group seeking a Mission Street franchise. Chace was elected secretary. These changes signaled renewed talk by the company of plans to complete the Mission Street extension, as reported July 5, 1890, by the *Surf*:

"The money subscribed as a fund for the extension of the Pacific Avenue street railway has now reached the sum of $2,700. Five thousand dollars is the sum asked for by the company. In a conversation with Thomas Cole, owner of the line, Mr. Cole said: 'It will cost at least $5,000 to build the road from Pope House to Garfield Park. Then there are, besides the expenses of equipment, of added taxation, added license, the longer line to keep in order, the greater cost of running so long a line and the fact that two or three years business at least will be a dead loss. If the road is extended it will be substantially built and well and thoroughly equipped. We shall give good and thorough service both winter and summer. The line will run from the present terminus at the Pope House out Mission Street to Younglove Avenue and thence via that avenue to the Tabernacle in Garfield Park. The Lower Plaza will then be the street railway center of the city. From the Plaza downward, past the beach to the mouth of the river and return will make a trip of 40 minutes' length. From the Plaza upward, through Mission Street and to the Tabernacle and return will also be a 40-minute trip. There will be three cars of lighter build provided for the hill travel and frequent trips will be made.

"'The winter service will also be thorough, giving those citizens living in the vicinity of Garfield Park and Mission Street ample facilities for reaching the business part of the town. In summer there will be a car every 20 minutes and in winter every 40 minutes. There will also be a car at 9 o'clock every evening giving an opportunity for shopping, calls, etc., and, if required, a car at the end of any large entertainment. A T rail will be laid at present, but as soon as travel justifies, a cable or an electric car will be established.'

"When asked if the line would not be extended to the Cliff road instead of Garfield Park, Mr. Cole replied that it would be impossible to give that distance for a five-cent fare, and therefore they would only build to the Park."

Despite these protestations, no work was started. Then, abruptly, the roof fell in. As described later, a new, dynamic company was formed in May 1891 to build an electric road from Garfield Park to the Lower Plaza and the beach. Cole countered May 30 with an announcement that San Francisco financier Anson P. Hotaling, builder of the Hotaling Block and owner of other local properties, was now interested in the Pacific Avenue company and intending to electrify the "yellow line." However, three days later, the Common Council gave franchises to the new company covering Mission Street above Walnut Avenue to Garfield Park, rights to share rails with the East Santa Cruz company on Front Street from Minnesota Avenue to the Lower Plaza, and a route to the beach out Cathcart Street, the Laurel Street extension, and Riverside Avenue, following the Pacific Avenue company's May 1888 charter. Cole's protests were ignored.

Work on the new electric road went rapidly. Some five months later, the first electric car ran from Pacific Avenue up Walnut, Mission, and Younglove Avenue to Garfield Park. Then the Cathcart-Riverside line was opened. Cole, Hotaling, and Younger had meantime applied to the Common Council for rights to electrify and were advised November 2 by the city attorney to proceed: that in his opinion their petition was unnecessary, the rights being vested in their present franchises. But the Common Council in February 1892 gave the new company yet another franchise, this time down Center Street from Walnut to the beach, paralleling "yellow line" service on Pacific Avenue. This completed an encirclement whereby the Pacific Avenue company was pinched off from expansion and threatened by direct competition to the beach.

It was time to throw in the towel, and this was done August 6, 1892, by sale of the Pacific Avenue company to the new interests. Reported the *Sentinel*: "When there was talk of changing the Pacific Avenue street railroad from horsepower to electricity, this newspaper earnestly advocated that it be made the same gauge as the electric road, as eventually the roads would be under one ownership as a financial necessity. It was also predicted that such would be the case. The prediction has been fulfilled in the purchase on Saturday of A.P. Hotaling's three-quarters interest in the Pacific Avenue road by J.P. Smith, who is the principal owner of the electric railway. Mr. Smith will probably electrify the road. He bought 750 shares, whose face value is $75,000. It is not known what he actually paid."

Electrification was indeed the plan. Horsecar service up Mission Hill ended in December, as the city made ready to regrade the hill. The tracks were removed. The retracking of Pacific Avenue began about March 1, 1893, with the rails temporarily spiked three feet apart to accommodate the horsecars. Service ended north of Walnut Avenue on March 13 and soon thereafter on the lower avenue. Cars, horses, and equipment of the Pacific Avenue company were offered for sale. By the end of April, the electrics were in full command, and horsecars along the avenue were only a memory.

13. Final Days for Horsecars

A CURIOUS anomaly had developed wherein the new horsecars of Ely's East Santa Cruz line were operating in the same time frame as the new electrics of the electric road. The *Surf* noted this disparity: "Wm. Ely was thought to be doing wonders to run a horse-car line to Twin Lakes a couple of years ago, but the horsecar is as far behind as the trail wagon now."

The horsecar company nonetheless carried 170,000 passengers in 1891, with receipts of $8,500 and expenses of $5,648. A small dividend was declared. Sylvar sold his stock and house to Bliss, his wife having died, and Eliza C. Beacon replaced Haslam as company secretary. The City Bank, Ely's bondholder, was named treasurer. Ely reported 14 cars and 15 horses operating over about four miles of track. The total cost for road and equipment thus far, he reported, had been $46,000.

In January 1892 Ely applied to the county supervisors for rights to use a "low-pressure steam motor engine" on his Twin Lakes branch. Several engines were being considered. Permission was given, but implementation was delayed. Meanwhile he put $4,500 more into upgrading the roadbed and obtained franchises for an extension up Ocean Street to the IOOF cemetery and a cross-river connection from Seabright to the Santa Cruz beachfront. Neither was built. The crash of 1893 ended such plans, as money became scarce and the building boom east of the San Lorenzo collapsed abruptly. Ely was left with a marginal horsecar operation and no immediate prospects for improvement.

With permission he abandoned service to Arana Gulch. Patronage had never justified this spur.

In April 1895 he renewed his petition for steam service, asking the Common Council for rights to operate a motor from the Lower Plaza to Ocean Street, the east city boundary. The councilmen approved but on June 3, realizing they now had the necessary leverage, ordered Ely also to center his tracks in Front Street, conform them to the street grade, and macadamize Front Street from Cooper to the Lower Plaza. Ely consented and made ready to inaugurate the steam service. On June 28 a horsecar on the Twin Lakes line encountered the new motor, with the following results, as related in the *Surf:*

> "The East Santa Cruz car with a dilapidated white mare for a motor and the dark-skinned, black-haired man with a southern accent as motor man, came around the curve from Twin Lakes yesterday and confronted the new steam motor, 'Wm. Ely.'
>
> "'Wm. Ely' was temporarily off the track, but that was only because the employees had neglected to remove the encrusted earth and the prolific growth of mayweed and camomile which have gradually taken the rails in their close embrace during the regime of the old white mare. 'Wm. Ely' is all right—only a bit stiff in the joints from a long overland trip from Philadelphia and by this afternoon will no doubt be merrily spinning along the track with the entire rolling stock of the East Santa Cruz railway hitched on behind.
>
> "It was this that made the dark-eyed motorman sad. He apostrophized the old white mare a little mournfully—'Well, old feller, there won't be no use for you much longer. Your day's about over. This here steam motor's about done for you and you'll have to turn out to grass or go into a soap factory. Horses are about played out in this country anyhow.'"

On July 6 the "Wm. Ely" began service from the Lower Plaza to Twin Lakes, accompanied by the *Surf's* prediction that horsecars had now permanently passed from the Santa Cruz scene. But not quite. By October several East Santa Cruzans had petitioned the county supervisors to declare the diminutive motor a public nuisance. The supervisors ruled in November that Ely could operate the motor from Soquel Road to Twin Lakes but only twice daily on Soquel Road itself: morning and evening, from and to the carhouse. The motor must never be allowed to stand in Soquel Road. Back into service came the horsecars between Cayuga Street and the Lower Plaza.

Relocation of the Front Street tracks was not accomplished until midsummer 1897, at which time new ties were emplaced and the street macadamized. Service staggered along fitfully. The "Wm. Ely" was retired and the schedule to Twin Lakes sharply reduced, finally to one trip daily. Even this was halted in 1899. Pressed by the supervisors for information, Ely reported that the East Santa Cruz road had never paid much more than expenses for a single month and in some months "did not earn axlegrease." The supervisors, meeting in January 1900, chose not to revoke the franchise but rather to urge the restoration of service if possible.

It was not possible. Ely advertised the road for sale in April 1901, eliciting the following editorial comment from the *Surf:*

"Wm. Ely, for thirty years included in the list of prominent businessmen of Santa Clara, the builder of two business blocks and the owner of others, the builder of a street railroad, and an active man of affairs in general, has reached the point in life, where the sunset rays admonish him, that it would be wise to set his house in order. The era of expansion is past, the time for conservation of strength and energy and curtailment of business has come.

"Wm. Ely is a man accustomed for three score years and ten to making things move. He says now that he sees the moving time coming again for Santa Cruz, yet it is not his move. Wiser than many men, Mr. Ely decides to dispose of his property which stands in the path of progress and let younger men seize the opportunities. In placing his order for advertising the East Santa Cruz Railway, he says, 'Tell the people that I have pioneered the way for this road. I was ten years ahead of the times. This road holds the key to the De Laveaga Heights, the military encampment and the east side coast resorts. It ought now to be extended to the camp ground and could take in barrels of nickels this summer, but I am too old to undertake the work. It's time for me to sit on the porch and read the papers and watch the traffic pass by instead of carrying a crowbar and bossing a gang of men.

"'When I say I am willing to unload I mean it, and the price will be put at a tempting figure. I have been a hard-working man all my life. I am now 73 years of age. It is time for me to quit. I shall continue to run the mill and wood yard, but I must let go of bothersome things. I put $52,000 into this street railway and if times had continued prosperous as they were when it was started, it would have been a success, but as you

know everything fell flat here. Now a change has come, but it is for somebody else to take advantage of it. They may reap where I have sown. I am willing to sell at a figure which ought to tempt some capitalist to take hold of it. Street railways adequately equipped and properly run are one of the most profitable investments in the country and this can be made so, but the work must be done by a younger man. Tell all inquirers that I stand ready to make good on what I have said and will sell the property advertised at figures which will prove good investments for the purchasers.'

"There is no doubt that Mr. Ely means what he says," concluded the *Surf,* "and that on his bargain counter are offered some good buys, wherein idle money can be invested to advantage."

The advertisement itself was straightforward. "The East Santa Cruz Railroad. Runs from Lower Plaza to Twin Lakes, with spur to Arana Gulch. Two and four-fifths miles of tracks in good condition. Ninety-nine year franchise. Eight cars in good order with horses, car barns, and stable. Entire outfit at a bargain." Ely cleaned and cleared the Twin Lakes line in May 1901 and ran the advertisement periodically until August 1902 when a buyer appeared, ready not only to resurrect the Twin Lakes horsecar service but to push an electric road to Capitola. This development is discussed in 'The Electric Era.'

This might have been the end of horsecars in Santa Cruz, but it wasn't. There was one more: an "old gray mare" that pulled a car up into Laveaga Park, beginning in October 1908, from the end of the Water Street electric car line. Ex-conductor Edwin Yantis, interviewed by the *Sentinel's* Margaret Koch, vividly recalled this short-lived anomaly. "Those were easy-going days. Women brought their baby buggies aboard—we waited for them if they were approaching. No one hurried as we do today." The last driver was Elmer Emert—"just a kid," according to Yantis. Electrics supplanted this final horsecar in July 1910, when through service was inaugurated to the park's main gate.

ITS FRONT DASH thick with mud kicked up by the four-legged motive power, East Santa Cruz No. 4 stands in Soquel Road.
Randolph Brandt Collection

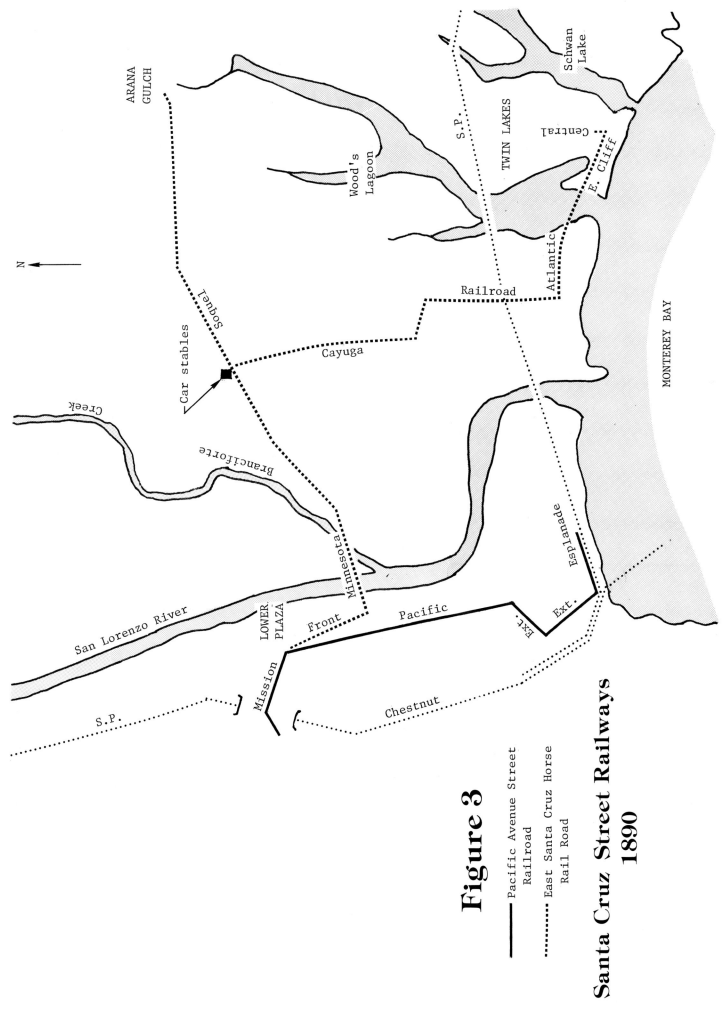

Figure 3

**Santa Cruz Street Railways
1890**

―――― Pacific Avenue Street
Railroad

∙∙∙∙∙∙∙∙ East Santa Cruz Horse
Rail Road

MONTEREY BAY

San Lorenzo River

S.P.

ARANA GULCH

Wood's Lagoon

Schwan Lake

TWIN LAKES

Central

E. Cliff

Atlantic

Railroad

S.P.

Soquel

Car stables

Creek

Branciforte

Cayuga

Minnesota

LOWER PLAZA

Front

Pacific

Mission

Chestnut

Ext.

Ext.

Esplanade

N

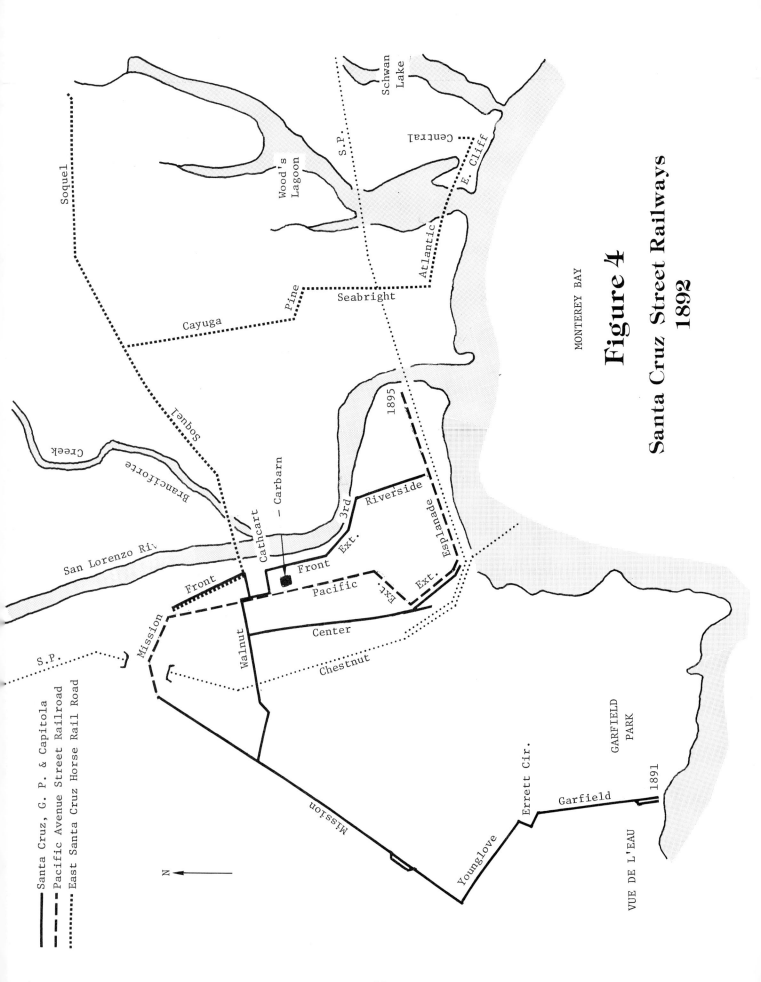

MONTEREY BAY

Figure 4
Santa Cruz Street Railways
1892

Wood's Lagoon

Schwan Lake

S. P.

Central

E. Cliff

Atlantic

Seabright

Pine

Cayuga

Soquel

Soquel

Creek

Branciforte

San Lorenzo Riv

Cathcart

Carbarn

1895

3rd

Riverside

Ext.

Front

Front

Pacific

Esplanade

Ext.

Ext.

Center

Mission

Walnut

Chestnut

S. P.

GARFIELD
PARK

Mission

Errett Cir.

Garfield

1891

Younglove

VUE DE L'EAU

N

Santa Cruz, G. P. & Capitola
Pacific Avenue Street Railroad
East Santa Cruz Horse Rail Road

34

Part 2

Electric Era

BY 1887 SANTA CRUZ was well established as a resort community and the financial center of Santa Cruz County. The economic storm clouds of the mid-1880s had blown away on the winds of fresh optimism. Newcomers flocked to the city. Land prices were climbing. Building was at an all-time high. Street improvements were under way, and strenuous efforts were being made to attract new industry.

These were exciting times. Summer brought throngs to the beaches, where Captain C.F. Miller had opened his Neptune Baths near the Leibbrandt bathhouses. A new resort, the Sea Beach Hotel, was under construction. Pope House had added to its laurels and so had Capitola—its hotel, burned out in the mid-1880s, was rebuilt and its founder, the venerable F.A. Hihn, was now even wealthier from Capitola land sales. Hihn had recently helped launch the Santa Cruz City Bank and City Savings Bank, serving both as vice-president. Deposits and loan activities at the banks were reported "brisk."

1. A Proposal

LOCAL INTEREST was now being focused on many innovations including the fledgling electric power industry sweeping the nation. Electricity was known to light cities, move transit systems, and power the wheels of industry. Thus it was in October 1887 that an electrical "expert," come to town to discuss electric street lighting, found a large and responsive audience. The expert was Frank Butterworth, general manager of the San Francisco Electrical Improvement Company, said to be the largest electrical contractor in the West and, coincidentally, engineers for the newly finished "underground electric" streetcar system in San Jose. Butterworth praised electric street lights and urged local businessmen to establish a power company. Then he got around to a favorite subject: electric traction.

Why not use electricity to move streetcars in Santa Cruz, he proposed. In San Jose, the new underground electric had recently carried 40,000 passengers in just one week (for the city's agricultural fair). The system had to be considered successful. How did it operate? Butterworth hastened to explain.

In San Jose, he said, streetcars on surface tracks drew electric power from a third rail suspended in an underground conduit. Mounted beneath the car was a carriage or "trolley" that rode the third rail through a slot in the street, resembling that of a San Francisco cable car track. Power from the third rail operated a motor in the car. Thus no electrical parts were exposed; dangerous rails and contacts were hidden well inside the conduit, out of reach by the general public.

Butterworth encouraged his listeners to build such a system in Santa Cruz. Total cost for tracks, rails, conduit, generator, steam plant, and four cars would not exceed $35,000, he was sure. The cars would move through the city streets at an average speed of 25 mph.

There was mild enthusiasm for the plan and even some talk about approaching the Common Council for a franchise, but no real action was taken. Two years later, when the San Jose system proved a disastrous $300,000 failure, local proponents for the underground electric must have breathed sighs of relief.

However, a seed was planted. There were many electrical advocates in Santa Cruz but, from the beginning, one of the staunchest (and most vocal) was young Fred Willer Swanton, Brooklyn-born son of local liveryman and hotelkeeper Albion P. Swanton. At age 27, young Swanton was already an experienced bookkeeper, realtor, hotel proprietor, druggist, and, above all, entrepreneur. In October 1889 he teamed up with Dr. H.H. Clark in an electric light business that was to bring them a fortune: capital stock worth $7,500 in 1889 was reportedly worth $100,000 in 1892. The two men invested heavily in real estate and other ventures, Swanton later coming to ownership of the beachfront Tent City company and promoting a variety of successful businesses.

The young man was also an advocate of electric power for streetcars and devoted considerable study to the subject, particularly to features of the overhead-wire system installed in San Jose in 1890 by banker James H. Henry. The engineers for this line were the Thomson-Houston Company of Boston, forerunners of General Electric and builders of streetcar systems in Seattle, Sacramento, and elsewhere.

CAR NUMBER ONE of the city's first electric streetcar company, the Santa Cruz, Garfield Park and Capitola, with its crew at Lower Plaza, foot of Front Street, in 1892. (Compare with view on Page 15.) *Charles Smallwood Collection*

2. The Electric Road

SWANTON'S aspirations got a boost in 1890 with the arrival of James Philip Smith and family from the East to make their home in Santa Cruz (he bought Kittridge House and remodeled it as his private residence). Smith, a wealthy businessman with interests in Paris and New York, brought to the community a special vitality and cosmopolitan outlook. The men struck up a firm friendship and mutual interest in Swanton's electric streetcar ideas, culminating in an organizational meeting May 19, 1891, "to consider an electric road": the time, 8 P.M., and the place, realtor Frank H. Parker's office on Pacific Avenue. Contingent on raising $20,000 in public subscription, the promoters firmed up plans for an electric road from the Lower Plaza to the beach, to the ocean cliffs beyond Garfield Park, and possibly even to Capitola. Subscribers pledged large sums. The need for public subscription had shrunk to $7,100 the following day, and May 21 brought word that the company would indeed organize.

This venture fitted perfectly with Swanton's ambitions. Since 1889, his *Santa Cruz Electric Light and Power Company*—he was general manager—had been serving a growing clientele. He had installed a 760-light Thomson-Houston generator and made other improvements to expand the company's capacity. Now he secured a contract to serve the new electric road if and when built.

On June 2, 1891, the Common Council passed ordi-

nances granting the new company rights to operate from the corner of Front and Minnesota out Walnut Avenue, Mission Street, Younglove Avenue, and Garfield Avenue (now Woodrow Avenue) to the cliffs and also from Front and Minnesota, up Front Street to the Lower Plaza, then out River Street to the north city boundary along the original franchise route of the Santa Cruz and Felton railroad. The first ordinance permitted shared rails with the Pacific avenue horsecar company and the second with Ely's East Santa Cruz horse railroad.

The electric road also got franchises that day for a route to the beach and a connecting line from the beach to Garfield Park, both sharing rails with the Pacific Avenue company if needed. The beach route was from Minnesota and Pacific Avenues down Pacific, Cathcart Street, Front Street extension, Laurel Street extension, and Riverside Avenue to the beachfront, thence westward to the foot of Pacific. The connecting line was from the foot of Pacific up Bay Street and out Lighthouse and Pelton Avenues to Garfield Avenue.

The total routes thus awarded by the four ordinances loosely described an apple-shaped system: from the north city boundary through the Lower Plaza to the corner of Minnesota and Pacific (the stem), thence down the riverbank to the beach, along the beachfront and cliffs to Garfield Park, and returning by way of Mission Street and Walnut Avenue to Minnesota and

Pacific. It was a *coup* for the electric road, lacking only a direct line to the beach down Pacific or an adjacent avenue to complete a monopoly on the profitable transit routes. As noted, it put great pressure on the management of the Pacific Avenue company.

The new road was incorporated June 5 as the *Santa Cruz, Garfield Park, and Capitola Electric Railway* with a 50-year life and capital stock of $100,000. In hand were subscriptions totaling $18,500, of which Smith had pledged $10,000, E.H. Robinson $2,500, Major Frank McLaughlin $1,000, and eight others (including Swanton and William T. Jeter) $500 apiece. Named directors were Smith, Robinson, Parker, Dr. Clark, Edward G. Greene, Judge J. Harvey Logan, and Frank W. Ely, California-born son of William and an established local furniture dealer. Among the subscribers and directors were some of the city's most influential citizens: McLaughlin a future mayor and chairman of the state's Republican Central Committee; Greene a former Vermont state legislator and now a city councilman; Logan president of the Bank of Santa Cruz and Savings and Loan Bank; and Jeter a future Santa Cruz mayor and then lieutenant-governor of California (1895-99), succeeding to the presidency of the Bank of Santa Cruz County. Logan and Jeter were to remain active in local transit affairs for many years.

The corporate charter described the preceding routes and also one from the corner of Front and Minnesota by the most practical means to Capitola, terminating near Hihn's resort hotel. The total length of all lines was estimated at 10 miles.

The local newspaper reported contracts went to Thomson-Houston for cars and equipment, specifying a 3'2" gauge with 35-pound T rail and 40-pound girder rail. This gauge choice relieved Smith and company of having to share tracks in Pacific Avenue with the horse-car company, whose 20-pound rail would not suffice for the electrics. Financing was obtained from San Francisco's First National Bank. Morris Newton of San Francisco, Smith's brother-in-law, took general charge of the construction, assisted by Frank Ely.

ALTHOUGH AIMING for the sleepy child, an early photographer fortuitously caught part of the electric railway carbarn on Pacific Avenue south of Cathcart Street. Cars entered and exited from Front Street, on the opposite side. *Randolph Brandt Collection*

The work began in July. A trestle was built in Front Street spanning the low-lying portions. A carbarn was erected on Pacific Avenue below Cathcart Street, with the cars entering at the rear from the trestle. By August 5, track was laid in Pacific Avenue from Cathcart to Walnut and the avenue repaved; poles were up along Mission Street near Walnut. The cars arrived from Stockton in September, equipped with both hand brakes and foot brakes. Trucks and motors were said to be on the way. On September 26 progress was reported satisfactory on all branches, with the electric road nearing completion. November 1 was chosen for ceremonies marking the first trial run.

OPEN BENCH electric car No. 6 awaits fare-payers at Vue de l'eau about 1895. Casino (right) was built in 1894. In distant background is the Christian Church tabernacle that opened in September 1890 and burned in August 1935. Note "Wye" switch that provided a two-car terminal. View looks down Garfield Avenue (now Woodrow Avenue).

Charles Smallwood Collection

VUE DE L'EAU CHALET is seen from two angles:

(ABOVE) From the spectacular ocean cliffs, the little structure appears at right. The view from the structure was equally superb.   *UCSC, Preston Sawyer Collection*
(BELOW) Behind the wooden frame structure sits a streetcar awaiting passengers for the return trip to city center.   *Randolph Brandt Collection*

All was in readiness for opening day. A terse announcement in the *Sentinel* preceded the event, and a reporter was on hand to witness the festivities:

"The prologue occurred on Sunday, November 1, 1891, when the first car of the electric railroad went over the Garfield Park branch to Vue de l'eau (at the end of Garfield Avenue). At 10:35 A.M. the observation car left the carhouse, the operating power being four black horses, with nickel-plated harness. Over the Front Street trestle the car glided smoothly along, and at the corner of Pacific Avenue and Cathcart Street it halted a few moments to take on invited guests. When it again started the following were among those who were on board: J.P. Smith, J.H. Logan, Morris Newton, Dr. H.H. Clark, E.H. Robinson, A.P. Swanton, S.B. Swanton, Wm. Ely, C.W. Waldron, R. Thompson, S.H. Bigland, Mayor Bowman, Dr. T.W. Drullard, F.W. Ely, E.C. Lilly, Z. Barnet, W.H. Roff, and C. Pioda.

"At 10:45 the car started up the avenue, and around the corner for half a block on Soquel Avenue, the moving evidence of progress gliding along. Then the horses were unhitched and attached to the opposite end of the car. The trip to Vue de l'eau was resumed. As the car continued up Pacific Avenue and into Walnut Avenue the progress of the car was watched by many people who lined the sidewalks."

The car successfully navigated Weeks' Hill on Walnut Avenue, halting briefly to pick up Weeks and then San Francisco banker James D. Phelan, who was hailed as he passed along the street. Next to board were Dwight W. Grover and his two children, and S.F. Grover. The car left the rails completely opposite Trescony Street, where the roadbed was not completely ballasted. Newton supervised getting it back on the tracks. About 11:30 it rolled up to Vue de l'eau for a victory celebration with champagne and cigars supplied by Phelan—a friend of Smith, mayor-to-be of San Francisco, and future U.S. senator from California. A flag was raised; infant Philip Smith Newton played a prominent role in the festivities. Toasts were drunk to Smith, Newton, and Judge Logan; to Phelan; and to S.G. Murphy, president of the First National Bank.

The car started back about 1:30. Santa Cruz, it was said, had now entered the electric era in earnest.

The company had hoped to inaugurate regular service early in November, but there were operating problems yet to be resolved. On one trial run, for example, a closed motor car with open observation trailer failed to navigate Weeks' Hill. The trailer was pushed back and, being empty, went off the track on the curve near the base of the hill. This problem was corrected by adjusting the current from the generator and installing a protective guardrail at the curve. A subsequent midnight trial run reached Vue de l'eau in just 16 minutes despite litter on the track that kept breaking the current.

Finally the line, generator, and rolling stock—two closed motor cars and two open trailers—were declared thoroughly in order. November 25 was chosen for the commencement of regular service, and a community barbeque was planned near the Vue de l'eau waiting station, a picturesque, pagoda-like structure.

"A gala day!" reported the *Surf* on November 26. "Promptly at 9 o'clock yesterday morning one of the motor cars of the electric railway started from in front of the company's office on Walnut Avenue for Vue de l'eau, the cliff terminus of the road. This was soon succeeded by the second car, and regular trips commenced at intervals of 20 minutes. Although one of the motors was not working to perfection, yet the runs were satisfactory and the cars glided over the route with an ease that was delightful to passengers and pleasing to the railroad

A SUMMER FAVORITE was this open-bench electric railway car.
UCSC, Preston Sawyer Collection

people. There was no lack of patrons from the start and the early trips made good returns on the conductors' cards, not to mention 'red' (complimentary) tickets which were freely used from the beginning.

"A car left Walnut Avenue every 20 minutes, meeting its mate on the return trip on the switch at Bay View. The run was made so easily that it was apparent that the round trip could be scheduled at one-half hour if necessity required.

"Before 11 o'clock the cars commenced to be crowded with passengers and by noon the scene at Pacific and Walnut Avenues was indicative of a street pageant. It was soon evident that the cars in operation were inadequate to convey the crowds to the barbeque grounds, and a long line of vehicles were soon en route.

"It was at this juncture that a breakdown occurred on the corner of Walnut Avenue and Mission Street, and electric locomotion was over for the day. F.W. Ely, who was on board the last car when the wheel crushed, was as prompt as a general on a battlefield and at once gave orders to engage all the buses and hacks in town and place them at the disposal of the people desiring to attend the barbeque."

Despite the breakdown, the line went into regular service as scheduled intending a 15-minute headway to Vue de l'eau but usually achieving about 20 minutes. Service opened down the Cathcart-Riverside route to the beach. The blue-and-white cars of the new electric road were crowded from dawn to dusk. The new road was proclaimed an unqualified success.

WHEN RIDING A TROLLEY was in style it was also the custom for the ladies to dress so as to prevent getting sunburned while at the seashore.
Harold Van Gorder Collection

3. Pacific Avenue Electrification

COLE, HOTALING, and associates had been told they could electrify their Pacific Avenue horsecar line but, on February 1, 1892, Smith and company countered by asking the Common Council for an alternate route to the beach: down Center Street from Walnut, paralleling the horsecar line. The right was granted February 11 with the proviso that the electric road lower its Front Street track to the city-approved grade. The new franchise put further pressure on the beleaguered Pacific Avenue management.

New open cars went into service on the electric road in March—"beauties," reported the *Sentinel*, "with an aisle down the center of each car."

The Center Street line opened for service (incorrectly ballasted, as later proved), but work to electrify Pacific Avenue was not begun. The reason became obvious in August with sale of the Pacific Avenue company, as previously decribed, to Smith and his partners. On August 19 Smith declared the electric road to be profitable, having carried 125,000 passengers during a recent "encampment week." The total investment thus far, including purchase of the Pacific Avenue line, was $180,000. The latter would have new rails and ties, and its electrification would cost at least $30,000 more. Six new cars would be used on the avenue. Smith said he expected the work to be completed by spring.

Smith also urged a $50,000 bonus from Capitola interests to help defray the expected $150,000 expense for extending the electric road to that community. On receiving this, he told the *Sentinel*, the line would be built.

The two companies merged August 23 to form the *Santa Cruz Electric Railway* with a 50-year term and capital stock of $500,000 ($10,500 subscribed, including $7,500 by Smith). Seven directors were named, among them Smith, Logan, Frank Ely, Dr. Clark, and Newton. Abandoned from the corporate charter were the Lighthouse-Pelton route and River Street. Added, however, was the Pacific Avenue franchise: from Mission and Walnut up Mission and down Pacific to the beach, thence to the mouth of the San Lorenzo River.

Judge Logan was installed as the first (and only) president of the Santa Cruz Electric Railway. Frank Ely was named general manager. On September 27 the officers authorized a bonded indebtedness of $280,000, later ratified by the shareholders. Only $60,000 was actually borrowed.

Urged by counsel, the new company then approached the Common Council for specific permission to electrify the Pacific Avenue line. Reported the *Surf*: "There was quite an animated session at the Council last evening (October 3) and a considerable municipal business transacted, the most important being the passage of an ordinance granting Messrs. Smith, Logan and Ely a franchise to build and operate an electric car line over the route of the present Pacific Avenue Street Railroad. . . . The ordinance passed last night is more carefully drawn than any that have been previously granted and to all appearances is designed to well protect the public interest. C.B. Younger was present and protested against its passage, but it was finally adopted by a unanimous vote, excepting Mr. Greene, who declined to vote for the reason that he is a stockholder in the electric road."

Formal acceptance was delayed by the company some three weeks while Smith and associates studied the terms. Finally, on October 27, the company agreed with minor revisions. City ratification followed soon thereafter.

Plans were made to start the work in January or February, after the winter rains. Beach service would be maintained down the other routes. Meanwhile the company proceeded with other improvements, building a spur track to the railroad depot from Sycamore Street and installing double trucks on the cars. The rolling stock and facilities were inspected on invitation in late November by H.A. Iddings, manager of San Francisco's Metropolitan Electric Railway. He complimented the working of the new Bemis trucks and also the brakes. He also admired the switches, which were

SANTA CRUZ ELECTRIC open car (far right) meets a South Pacific Coast train at Union Station. Also waiting are horse-drawn wagons of the Santa Cruz Transfer Express Company and from the Ocean Villa Hotel. Electric cars and hotel "buses" met most trains. *Ayelotte Photo UCSC, Preston Sawyer Collection*

CLIMBING MISSION HILL in the mid-1890s, Santa Cruz Electric No. 6 passes handsome Mission Hill School. *Randolph Brandt Collection*

of Santa Cruz manufacture, and the transfer table, which was of Ely's design.

The city began grading Mission Hill in December. Horsecar service was suspended at the Lower Plaza, as previously noted, and the track was removed from the hill.

In January 1893 Ely ordered the materials for retracking Pacific Avenue: 126 tons of 40-pound combination rail, 23,000 spikes, nearly 6,000 bolts, and many other items including about 4,000 ties. Also ordered were 210 poles and approximately four tons of electric wire. Ely estimated the cash outlay at around $25,000. Grover and Company got the lumber contract and bought a mill near Boulder to facilitate deliveries.

Work started early in February. Arrangements were made to share poles along Pacific Avenue south of Maple with the light company and with the Sunset Telephone Company. By month's end track had been laid in Mission Street from Walnut Avenue to the top of Mission Hill; the crews were ready to move into Pacific Avenue. Pole erection was also proceeding

ELECTRIC RAILWAY closed car passes Sea Beach hotel shortly after electrification of the Pacific Avenue horse-car line. *Harold Van Gorder*

swiftly, now finished along Mission from Walnut to the hill and commencing in the avenue.

However, a problem had arisen. Winter rains washed out the ballast under the Center Street line down near the beach, halting electric car service for at least three weeks to effect repairs. Immediate suspension of the horsecars would end service to the depot and wharf area. So Ely elected to gauge the new track temporarily at three feet in Pacific Avenue to accommodate the horsecars while the repairs were in progress.

Trucks and motors arrived in Santa Cruz March 10 for converting the trail cars into motor cars for the expanded service. It was speculated that the Pacific Avenue horsecars might be used as trail cars by the electric, although Ely had by now offered them for sale. One report claims they were briefly used on the Center Street line during the mid-1890s.

On March 13 crews began regauging the Pacific Avenue track to 3'2". Horsecar service stopped at Walnut Avenue. Graders went to work south of Walnut while construction north of the corner was pushed to completion, the first electric car running through the Lower Plaza and up Mission Hill to Vue de l'eau on April 1. Regular service began the following day with a 40-minute headway, alternating with cars of the Walnut Avenue branch to provide 20-minute service from Walnut and Pacific to Vue de l'eau. Walnut Avenue was temporarily shut down in April for minor repairs. Both lines were operating again by May 2.

Meanwhile, south of Walnut, electric service commenced in the avenue April 6 to the Cottage Saloon, near Beach Hill. Six days later the cars reached a point opposite the train depot, from which a new spur line was built to the depot. The running time from here to Vue de l'eau was 30 minutes. On April 22 electric service opened to the Sea Beach Hotel, and by month's end the line was completed to its beachfront terminus at the bathhouses.

FIRE! Santa Cruz Electric No. 7 passes smouldering ruins after the disastrous April 1894 blaze that leveled most of downtown Santa Cruz.

UCSC, Preston Sawyer Collection

4. Feast, Famine, and Fire

IT WAS NOW time for consolidating the gains and acquiring practical operating experience with the expanded road. One of the first matters was scheduling. "Manager Ely is busily making out time schedules in anticipation of the completion of the track and finds the task anything but an easy one," reported the *Surf* in early April. "This paper would like to whisper to passengers that the proper thing is to await the car on a street corner and not expect the motorman to drive up to the sidewalk anywhere they may choose to stop. The irregular stoppages throw the car out of time badly."

The company soon followed with a blunter message. "Santa Cruz Electric Railway has made it a rule on and after today," it advised on April 14, "that stops will be made on street corners only. The company desires to give the public the best possible service and hopes that all patrons will assist them in their efforts by cheerfully complying with their request to 'Wait on the Corner for the Car.'"

With all lines in operation, Ely established 20-minute headway from the beach, Minnesota and Pacific, and Vue de l'eau, the latter alternating between the Mission Hill and Walnut Avenue branches. The first car was 6:20 A.M. and the last around midnight. Service was less frequent after 6 P.M., although special cars were dispatched for well-attended evening activities. Arrangements were made to meet the early-morning train

(6:40 A.M.) and other arrivals, by stationing a car on the spur track at the depot.

Some minor operating problems developed. In late March the company offered $25 for information leading to the identification of the party or parties— "probably boys"—who had put rocks and sticks between the rail and guardrail on Weeks' Hill, derailing an upbound electric car and delaying traffic for more than an hour. "It could have been far worse if downward bound," the *Surf* declared.

Electrical malfunctions interrupted service: generator failures, downed wires, etc. In April, car service was suspended one evening to accommodate the removal of a private residence (the trolley and guide wires had to be cut). And the public had to get accustomed to the new system, as evidenced by the following account— titled "Electrified"—from the *Surf:*

"A young man of this city, one of the alleged bright set, had a little experience Tuesday evening which he will not soon forget. This young man had gone to see his 'best girl' who lives somewhere on the electric car line. He seemed quite intent upon creating a favorable impression with the young lady and, as bright boys do, proceeded to cut up all sorts of antics. One of these was catching hold of a wire, which was dangling from an electric light post, and swinging himself to the top of a nearby fence. He had performed this feat successfully a number of times, when, in some unaccountable manner, the wire came in contact with the trolley wire of the electric railway. Again he swung himself fenceward, but much to his surprise, and it may be said pain, he found himself landed on

44

LOTS OF FRESH AIR cools the passengers aboard Santa Cruz Electric Railway car No. 5. This company succeeded the Santa Cruz, Garfield Park and Capitola after acquisition of the Pacific Avenue horsecar company.
Harold Van Gorder Collection

the small of his back in a mud hole; he attempted to rise, but that wire was loaded for bear, and he was thrown in the mud again, this time face down. He finally broke away, however, and, leaving his girl gazing more or less affectionately after him, he rushed down the street homeward, where he arrived a sadder and, it is to be hoped, a wiser young man."

Opening an extension of Front Street (the company had hoped to offer through service from the Lower Plaza down the riverbank line through this street) was halted when the Fair Association, owner of a key land parcel in its path, voted against the plan. Minor pressures developed in the community for wider streets, better paving, and improved grades all to be accomplished at company expense (uniformly resisted by the company). Eventually demanded was the removal of tracks from Center Street, service having been sharply curtailed along this route with the opening of the Pacific Avenue line.

Nonetheless, the new electric road proved immensely popular. On Sunday, July 2, 1893, the proceeds for just that day came to 10,275 nickel fares. "This figures car receipts of $50 an hour," marveled the *Surf*. "Not even the wildest dreamer could have predicted this, two years ago."

This was feast time for the Santa Cruz Electric. Then came the 1893 crash with its capital shortage and collapse of the building boom. This was followed in April 1894 by Santa Cruz's most devastating fire, which opened Front Street but at the opposite end from that expected. "There is no longer a Chinatown in Santa Cruz," reported the *Sentinel* somberly. "From opposite Cooper Street to River Street, on the east side of Front Street, not a building is standing." The loss was said to be staggering.

The fire started about 10 P.M. Saturday, April 14, the flames being spotted at 10:40 shooting from the rear of E.L. Williams' real estate office and Werner Finkeldey's grocery on Cooper Street. Fanned by a stiff north wind, the conflagration spread to Wessendorf and Staffler's undertaking rooms and Mike Leonard's two-story wooden building on the corner, then jumped the street to the 27-year-old brick courthouse.

By 3 A.M. the east side of Pacific Avenue was engulfed in flames. Frank Ely transferred most of his furniture business to the electric car barns, thus suffering minimum damage. Other merchants saved what they could. Many buildings were destroyed and others completely gutted, such as Hotaling's three-story business block and John Werner's white-fronted building on Pacific. With the morning light, confronting the weary firefighters was a stretch of rubble-filled basements and partly standing brick walls. Of the People's Bank and the City Bank, only their brick vaults remained.

Individual losses were appalling. Werner estimated $17,000, J.F. Simpson $15,000, and C.B. Pease $10,000. Hotaling's loss was put at $50,000 with insurance of only $10,000. The City Bank was similarly underinsured: $25,000 loss versus $10,000 insurance.

A CLEAR DAY IN 1895. Santa Cruz Electric No. 3 runs along lower Pacific Avenue. A new carbarn was later built at Pacific and Sycamore, first street to the left.
UCSC, Preston Sawyer Collection

ALONG SANTA CRUZ'S BEAUTIFUL BEACH, an open-bench electric car carries an overflow load towards the resorts. Bedell House (see banner on near end of streetcar) was a fashionable retreat on Mission Street beyond Pope House. Along the boardwalk, outside the Southern Pacific, is the track of the Santa Cruz, Capitola and Watsonville electric railway, curving around to its terminus, where passengers are waiting.

Morris Photo, Randolph Brandt Collection

The streetcar company suffered only minor damage, its carhouse, generators, and rolling stock being out of the path of the flames. Lines went down and debris covered the track in Pacific Avenue. By Sunday evening, however, the obstructions had been removed; service was restored the following morning.

Thus Santa Cruz—and the immediate fortunes of Smith and company—passed from feast to famine in a few short months. Plans for the Capitola extension were scrapped. Instead the company devised some lesser objectives.

One was building the city's first casino, which opened in 1894 at Vue de l'eau. It was advertised as a wholesome family resort with a ballroom on the second

floor, restaurant and lounge on the first floor. Offices and storerooms occupied the upper story. A broad porch ran around the structure, behind which was a baseball diamond where the company's team, the Electrics, gained local fame. George Denison, veteran hotelman of Santa Cruz and the San Lorenzo Valley, ran the facility. One of his early-day advertisements promised: "My patrons will find the Casino a first-class family resort. Special attention given to dancing, dinner and lunch parties."

In 1895 the electric road was extended along the beachfront from the bathhouses to the San Lorenzo river, duplicating service of the past decade by the Pacific Avenue horsecar company. The city built a dam

across the river near its mouth, backing up the water to create a lagoon. A footbridge was built across the river to serve residents of East Cliff and Seabright.

In 1896 the company reported eight motorcars and seven miles of line. The funded debt was still $60,000. President of the road was Judge Logan with Smith vice-president, Jeter secretary, and Ely general manager and purchasing agent. Serving now as treasurer was the Bank of Santa Cruz County. Ely resigned soon thereafter, moving to Paso Robles and eventually to a furniture association with Breuner's in Oakland. His replacement was E.S. West, former superintendent of the Pacific Avenue company.

Smith, now often dubbed "Silent Jim" because of his demeanor or "Sunshine Jim" because of converting Kittridge House into Sunshine Villa, poured a lot of money into the community during these years. He made possible the Venetian water carnivals of 1895-96 when the San Lorenzo lagoon sported many decorated and illuminated festival craft. He built a dancing pavilion at Pacific Avenue and Laurel Street which, as the Palm Theater, burned November 24, 1897. It had the distinction of playing Santa Cruz's first movies, on December 28, 1896, when flicker scenes showed a New York city street and a ferryboat in motion.

The Smith and Fred Swanton homes were centers of the Santa Cruz social whirl in this decade, famous for their hospitality and the elegance of their parties.

The electric road made a major equipment improvement early in 1897 involving its inner workings rather than its outer trappings. During the previous year Swanton and others had organized a new company to produce electric power from water flowing down Big Creek Canyon from the Santa Cruz Mountains. This project—the *Big Creek Power Company*—was Swanton's most ambitious thus far. Money was raised and a plant built. Swanton then astonished local builders by pushing 18 miles of power line from the plant in just 60 days. Now he sought to supply power for the Santa Cruz streetcars.

PLEASURE-SEEKERS alight from SCE No. 6 at Tent City Restaurant, Beach and Cliff Street, in 1904. The building bore a "Ladies Entrance" sign, an indication of the customs of the time. The "Plaza Only" roofboard on the streetcar indicated that this car was in shortline service from the beach to the plaza.
Randolph Brandt Collection

Smith and the company agreed. Changes to the car-house began in February 1897. Foundations for two generators and a big electric motor were laid the following month. Then, on Friday, April 9, all was in readiness.

"Invisible power passes from water wheels on Big Creek by electric current to car wheels on Pacific Avenue," declared the *Surf* the next day. "After many delays and disappointments the electric motor, which is to transform the electric power from the Big Creek line into shape to operate the Santa Cruz Electric Street Railway, arrived Thursday morning. A mere turn of the band Friday afternoon sent the cars of the Santa Cruz Electric Railroad gliding along their course by the power of the stream which has gone tumbling down its rocky course in the Big Creek Canyon for thousands of years, in wanton idleness.

"The genius of Edison and Tesla, the energy of F.W. Swanton, and the money of the Big Creek Power Company have combined to accomplish a result that is really inspiring in its conception.

"The new motor at the car house was put in position and connected in the forenoon under the direction of Mr. R.S. Masson of the Westinghouse Company. At 2:30 in the afternoon, a whistle indicated that the transmission and transmutation of power was complete, and without a hitch or tremor the transition was made, and it was—a success."

This was the most dramatic change of the late 1890s. Then followed retrenchment. Service was halted to the river mouth and curtailed on the Riverside Avenue line. The Center Street line was abandoned and the rails removed. In 1899 cars stopped running on the Walnut Avenue branch. These were for reasons of economy. Elsewhere the company acceptably maintained its roadbed, equipment, and service, its directors firmly in command of the local situation and eyeing their prospects benignly. As events proved, their vision was short-sighted.

LOOKING DOWN FROM BEACH HILL, Santa Cruz Electric No. 6 is seen in lower Pacific Avenue.
Harold Van Gorder Collection

NESTLED AMONG THE PALMS, an SCE car awaits passengers at its beachfront terminus. In the background is Sea Beach Hotel. This photograph dates to 1900.
Harold Van Gorder Collection

ENTERING CAPITOLA, electric car No. 14 turned right just beyond the bridge into the Esplanade, continued two blocks to Bay Avenue (now Monterey Avenue), looped past Hotel Capitola, and returned to the bridge via Capitola Avenue.

Randolph Brandt Collection

5. Birth of the Capitola Electric

THE TWENTIETH century opened quietly enough with local announcement that the *Bay and Coast Railroad,* successors to the *West Coast Railway Company,* was seeking rights for a coast railroad from San Francisco to Santa Cruz, ultimately to reach Monterey. This was old hat; similar schemes had been advanced locally for decades. The county supervisors voted January 20 not to revoke William Ely's horsecar franchise to Twin Lakes even though Ely had stopped running cars. This, too, suggested business as usual.

The first big news of the century broke in February with sale of the Big Creek Power Company by Swanton and colleagues to F.W. Billing and John Q. Packard, prominent mine investors from Utah. The price was $250,000, and the agent for the transaction was capitalist James W. Forgeus, recently arrived in Santa Cruz to set up a business in Cooper Street "buying real estate, bonds, stocks, mortgages, and selling same." Here was a veteran promoter ostensibly come to the seashore for "a few years of simple living, restoring a somewhat shattered state of health." The *Surf* later described him as "a doer and a money-maker. That is his standard of attainment. . . . He is quick of thought, speedy of action, and as void of patience as Rockefeller's head is

of hair. He is possessed of a copious vocabulary of expletives, and he does not hesitate to exhaust the stock in characterization of certain local capitalists whom he finds it difficult to do business for, with or against."

One immediate effect of the sale was to supply Swanton fresh capital for other pursuits (he soon launched a local oil promotion). Of more consequence, it put him in touch with a new breed of investors—Forgeus, Packard, and others—who were willing to risk vast sums if need be to gain their ends. Tough, venturesome, and experienced infighters, they were well suited to the task of consolidating utilities, transit systems, and the like into combines many of which exist today. Swanton studied their methods and liked their game. He was ready to play if bigger interests moved into Santa Cruz.

Peace reigned during 1900 and 1901 although the local newspapers were full of reports about transit mergers elsewhere. Oakland's surface lines were consolidated. Baltimore industrialists bought several Bay Area properties, supposedly part of a scheme to build an electric road from San Francisco to San Jose. Up in Marin County, the North Shore—backed by powerful electric utility interests—was spending hundreds of thousands on a third-rail system out of Sausalito. Down south, Bakersfield was completing an electric railway, and Henry E. Huntington was pouring millions into his Pacific Electric empire that also included utilities. The *Sentinel* urged a merging of local interests to put the electric railway, power company, lighting company, and Ely horsecar road under the same management. There was no public response. Actually a larger scheme was already underway privately, masterminded by Swanton.

March 1902 brought word from nearby Gilroy that an electric light franchise had been given in that city to a company headed by Mr. Smith and Mr. Gardiner, who were negotiating also to buy the Gilroy Gas Light Company. "It is rumored that this is the same company that recently purchased the Salinas City Light and Power Company's plant," explained the *Surf.* "They will

Gradually the story unfolded. Gardiner and associates had been contacting principals from Bakersfield to San Jose, focusing mainly on the central coast counties of Santa Cruz, Monterey, San Benito, and San Luis Obispo. Swanton had meanwhile quietly picked up Ely's East Santa Cruz railroad bonds from the City Bank, gaining control over this valuable franchise route toward Capitola, Watsonville, and Monterey. Swanton controlled the light company and had entry through Forgeus to the Big Creek Power Company. He made it known that he would like to meet the Gardiner people.

The meeting took place. Negotiations began around March for the syndicate to buy Santa Cruz Electric Light and Power. Swanton learned then of their interest not only in buying and electrifying the East Santa Cruz railroad but also in electrifying the Monterey and Pacific Grove horsecar road, miles from Santa Cruz at

THE CENTER OF CAPITOLA was graced by Frederick A. Hihn's 160-room Hotel Capitola. This hostelry became the eastern terminus of the Santa Cruz, Capitola and Watsonville electric railway promoted by Fred Swanton and the "Gardiner Syndicate," actually a front for H.M. Byllesby and Co. of Chicago.
Randolph Brandt Collection

construct a new plant in Monterey, while Watsonville and Santa Cruz are on the list of towns they wish to control." Backing Smith and Gardiner was said to be none other than Henry Huntington.

The shopping list was essentially correct. Huntington's backing was not. "Mr. Smith" was really R.C.P. Smith, a Los Angeles banker with growing utility holdings in Southern California. "Mr. Gardiner" was John M. Gardiner, a respected promoter and developer from the southland. Their "company" was a syndicate also including O.Z. Hubbell and banker Martin V. McQuigg from Ontario in San Bernardino County. These men, soon known locally as the "Gardiner syndicate," were in fact fronting for H.M. Byllesby and Company, a Chicago-based utility investment firm with large holdings in the Midwest. Byllesby intended to diversify to the West Coast; several teams like Gardiner's were reportedly at work in California buying transit systems and gas, electric, and water companies.

the other end of Monterey Bay, recently bought for that purpose. McQuigg was an incorporator and financier of this company. The Gardiner group wanted to connect the two roads and build a branch line to Salinas, with the goal eventually of promoting a coastal electric railway from San Francisco to Monterey.

Swanton pledged his support and sold the light company. The announcement came on May 5. "The Santa Cruz Electric Light and Power Company's plant, property and franchises in this city are under contract to be taken over within sixty days by Messrs. Hubbell, Smith and Gardiner of Los Angeles, the parties who have recently acquired gas works, electric light plants and street railroads in several California towns. . . . The revenues of the Santa Cruz company have been examined and its property inspected, and a price agreed upon. The purpose of the new concern is by introducing modern methods to cheapen the cost of production and to make substantial reduction in cost to consumers. Their

APPROACHING HOTEL CAPITO-
LA, Capitola electric car No. 8 rolls
along the Esplanade, just east of San
Jose Avenue.

Harold Van Gorder Collection

Main Street. Capitola, Cal.

plans call for an expenditure of about $85,000 in new machinery, pipe, etc., provided that upon investigation the field promises to come up to their expectations."

The *Surf* speculated on the sale's implications. "When these people take up the electric light and gas proposition it is expected that they will take up the East Santa Cruz Street Railway . . . convert it into an electric railway and extend it to Capitola at once. Not in ten years has so much outside capital been hovering near Santa Cruz, and in no project could it be invested which would come so close home to the comfort and the pockets of so many people."

In August the speculation was confirmed. Engineers arrived to survey for a line eastward from Twin Lakes to Capitola. On September 11 the *Santa Cruz, Capitola and Watsonville Railway Company* was born, incorporated for 50 years with a capital stock of $350,000 and pledges of $100,000 divided equally among six men: McQuigg and Hubbell of Ontario; Gardiner of Pacific Grove; R.C.P. Smith of Los Angeles; hardware merchant and bank president Henry Willey of Santa Cruz; and Warren R. Porter of Watsonville, head of the Bank of Watsonville. The charter stipulated 20 miles of routes from Santa Cruz to Capitola and Watsonville to be operated by steam, electricity, or other motive power. It included the right to run steamboats.

Formal announcement of the incorporation came two days later. The board of directors consisted of Mc-Quigg, Gardiner, Willey, Hubbell, and Porter, the *Surf* declared, with McQuigg to be president. "Messrs. Willey and Porter are well known here as the presidents of local banks, and active and influential members of the community, politically and commercially. Mr. Gardiner is already known to many of business men, he having made the actual and practical examination of the territory, route and tributary business. It is now up to the citizens along the proposed routes to decide the way, as the directors state that they will make definite location of the route by the 10th of October." What this meant in practical terms was that the route would go where the citizens were most willing to sell (or give) their land and pay bonuses for the road's completion.

NO. 14 HALTS in Bay Street opposite Hotel Capitola.
Randolph Brandt Collection

H.M. BYLLESBY, electric utility and street railway magnate.
Minnesota State Archives

51

A company meeting September 20 authorized a bonded indebtedness of $75,000 and confirmed McQuigg as president with Gardiner vice-president and general manager, Smith secretary, and Porter treasurer. E.A. Cole was appointed superintendent.

The chief surveyor arrived in Santa Cruz from Los Angeles October 14 to fix the final route to Capitola. "The projectors of this road are anxious that interested property owners should decide at once whether they want it built or not," prompted the *Surf*. It was then revealed that McQuigg and Gardiner would leave soon for Cincinnati, Buffalo, St. Louis, and New York to buy cars and equipment for the Monterey electric and would also buy for the Capitola road if they decided before departing to build the road. That did the trick. Subscriptions poured in, and the necessary equipment was ordered.

With Swanton fronting for the new company, the Common Council on December 17 gave it operating rights from the corner of Front and Soquel to the depot via Soquel and Pacific Avenues, Lincoln Street, Center Street, and the Washington Street extension. This was followed January 5, 1903, by an ordinance permitting electrification of the Ely railroad: Front Street from the Lower Plaza to Soquel Avenue, then out this avenue to the east city boundary. On February 16 rights were given to operate south from the depot along Pacific Avenue to 10 feet south of the Southern Pacific tracks, then eastward 1123.2 feet along the beachfront by single track with no switches or turnouts.

The county supervisors also moved with dispatch, passing an ordinance January 6 that allowed electrification of Ely's Twin Lakes and Arana Gulch franchise routes. The maximum fare would be 5¢ from the city boundary to Twin Lakes. In these franchises—city and county—the company was given a choice of flat or T rail and any gauge from 36 to 56½ inches. The maximum speed in all cases was 20 mph. Switches and turnouts were forbidden except at street junctions unless otherwise specified. The city franchises carried an extra proviso that police officers and city employees in performance of their duties must be carried free.

Grading for the new road was well under way by mid-February, occasioning the following lengthy report by the *Surf*:

"There is considerable work to be done on the old horse car route on curves and crossings, but no material change until Twin Lakes is approached. The grade at the westerly end of the bridge crossing Wood's Lagoon is being lowered and at the opposite end of this bridge the new road abandons the Ely grade and takes as near a straight line as may be for the bluff on the easterly side of the second lagoon. This involves a fill of perhaps 200 yards of sand and earth before reaching the Twin Lakes station.

"The dirt and sand for this fill is being transported on cars constructed under the direction of Mr. Fuller (chief engineer for the city of Santa Cruz), with the trucks of the old horsecars as a foundation. On the floor of the car is built up a box with a partition in the middle, the sides being falling doors, so to speak. Fastened in place, the car is loaded, then run over the track to its destination, the sides let down, the dirt falls by its own gravity, and there you are. One of these cars accomplishes as much in way of transportation as seven or eight teams hauling wagons.

"The new line in front of Twin Lakes boldly strikes across the beach at the highest point that the tide touches. A box drain will provide outlet for the lake, and also inlet for the salt water at high tide Considerable cutting of the cliff will be required at this point and the material will form a top dressing for the sand fill across the beach. Soon after this eminence is gained, the trolley line will turn directly north and follow a street to the main road now leading from Twin Lakes to Santa Maria del Mar. This road at present is rolling, but an agreement has been reached with Supervisor Collins whereby it is to be put on a uniform grade, the cost to be divided between the railway company and the county. George Pratcher is the foreman of a gang of teams, plows and scrapers at work at this place.

"At the point where the new highway, opened last year, leads off to the Soquel road, the electric right of way leaves the county road and enters lands of Corcoran, running along the northerly side of the hedge which bounds the Del Mar property. Reaching Corcoran's lagoon a deflection is made northerly for a few hundred feet to an arm of the lagoon which is to be crossed on a fill. For several days the ooze absorbed the dirt as fast as it was dumped, but solid bottom has now been reached and the fill is progressing satisfactorily.

"Crossing a point of land the projection of the main lagoon is encountered. About 80 feet of trestle will be introduced here, with filled approaches. We did not count, nor inquire, but should judge that as many as ten four-horse teams were at work at this point, and considerable of an embankment has been raised."

The *Surf* also described plans for a new Santa Cruz beachfront esplanade along which the car track would be built:

"This is to extend from the wharf to the Mills Building on the beach, a distance of a little over 1,100 feet, with a uniform width of 35 feet. Of this a clear space of 23 feet will extend from the car track to the front facing the bay, for a promenade.

"The plans contemplate a line of piling along the water front, about six feet of planking, to extend to the sand. Back of this redoubt against the tide, the space is to be filled with sand. For the present season it is proposed to cover this with cinders well rolled. After allowing time to settle, a bituminous rock pavement is to be spread. A balustrade of iron posts and rails, or chains will protect the pedestrian on the seaward side. Two street ways cross this explanade and the plans include proper approaches for the streets.

"The offer of the railway company . . . is to pay two-thirds of the cost of construction of this esplanade, the city to pay the balance. The railway company will abate that portion of their franchise . . . which involves the right to construct turn tables, switches, etc., continuing it as a simple right of way."

Fired by local enthusiasm and unrestrained thus far by the older Santa Cruz Electric, the new company pressed its advantage. Early in February its management sent out postcards urging the property owners along Water and Ocean Streets to endorse a branch passing through those streets to the IOOF cemetery. The response was positive. On February 25 it asked the Common Council for operating rights from the end of Front Street through the Lower Plaza, across the Water Street "upper bridge," and out Water and Ocean to the cemetery, a distance of about 1½ miles. Supporting the request was a petition from the owners of "more than five-eighths of the real property fronting along and upon the route of this franchise." It was promptly granted.

Then the Capitola road asked rights for Pacific Avenue from Lincoln Street northward to the Lower Plaza, invading the franchise of the Santa Cruz Electric. The peace was over. Officials of the older line rolled up their sleeves to square off against the intruder.

6. Battle of the Five Blocks

A FRANK appraisal was in order. The Santa Cruz Electric was a valuable property: adequately financed, well maintained, and well patronized. Recently it had introduced "short line" service for cars up bound from the Lower Plaza, those with blue flags continuing on to Vue de l'eau while those with red flags stopped in Mission Street opposite Bedell House. This doubled the frequency of cars in Pacific Avenue. Aging owner J. Philip Smith, a local legend because of his philanthropies, had now quit Santa Cruz in favor of Paris, but he and the other directors, especially Judge Logan, still enjoyed the community's highest esteem.

The Capitola road for its part had strong financial backing, momentum, and an aggressive management including Willey, Porter, and Swanton, all likewise of high local esteem. The community generally supported development of this road; many city and county officials, as well as a large number of private citizens, stood to benefit in various ways from its completion. The "foreign" interests behind the road—Gardiner and associate—were dedicated to acquisitions through purchase or merger, as demonstrated by events of the past year. Some sort of bid could be expected sooner or later for the Santa Cruz Electric.

Smith, Logan, and colleagues were not reluctant to give up their road if the terms were right. The crux of their problem was to maintain its value in the face of a frontal assault. Three strategies were indicated: resistance in the Common Council, resistance if need be in the courts, and improvements in service to increase ridership or gain strategic advantage. The essential first step was to plead their cause before the public, soliciting what criticisms of the new road that might develop.

Thus, starting in late March 1903, the *Sentinel* and *Surf* began publishing letters criticizing the Capitola road. For a $1 franchise fee, complained "A Taxpayer," the city is providing $2,000 to build a railroad station and esplanade for the benefit of the streetcar company. "Pacific Avenue" condemned the Common Council for allowing the new company, under terms of its Water-Ocean franchise, to haul freight over the city streets. Several editorials invoked the spectre of two streetcar companies operating over the same rails or side by side in Pacific Avenue, congesting that thoroughfare. "The Santa Cruz, Capitola and Watsonville can reach the beach from the Lower Plaza via Front, Soquel, Lincoln and Center streets," explained the *Surf.* "The route is not equivalent to Pacific Avenue, but the distance between the lines would be short, not exceeding 1,100 feet."

The *Surf* also published a long letter by "Pacific Avenue" laying down the Santa Cruz Electric's legal objections to a second franchise on the avenue. The mayor and council were wrong, insisted the writer, even to consider the petition of the Capitola Road. Supposedly they were acting according to provisions of Section 499 of the Civil Code, 1891 amendments, that allowed two different companies to use the same street for no more than five consecutive blocks, each paying an equal portion for the construction of tracks and appurtenances used jointly by the two companies. But these provisions no longer applied. "The right of the Mayor and Common Council to refuse to grant any franchise applied for is unquestioned," the writer concluded. "It is clearly a matter of discretion. . . . It is contended that this law is repealed by the act providing for the sale of franchises, and if this contention is correct, there is no authority vested in the Council to grant the permit to use the track of the Santa Cruz Electric Railway."

The debate spread to the Common Council chambers where, on April 6, arguments were heard that Pacific Avenue was too narrow for two railroads. C.B. Younger, now nearing his seventieth year, rose to support these arguments, insisting that J. Philip Smith had spent $150,000 to $200,000 in developing the Santa Cruz Electric and this investment would now be jeopardized. The councilmen stoically observed that, by law, they could not deny the franchise. Having so declared, they opened sealed bids as now also required by law, receiving one for $1,000 from a C.J. Dondero, one for $500 from a J. Lennon of San Francisco, and one for $200 from Fred Swanton. The award went to Dondero. This, too, was legally required. Then Swanton capped the evening's merriment by asking for a new franchise on Pacific from Lincoln to the Lower Plaza, differing only in that it described a curve through the Lower Plaza connecting with the Front Street track of the Capitola Road. The petition was duly received and everybody went home.

Dondero did not return April 8 for his franchise, so it went to Lennon. He, also, failed to appear, so it went to Swanton. That was on April 9. Swanton's second franchise also came up for hearing that evening. Supposedly this would be perfunctory, but R.C.P. Smith showed up with a second request covering exactly the same route. The *Sentinel* was piqued. "Up to the time of adjournment," it pondered, "no one had answered the question, 'Who is R.C.P. Smith?' Who are all these people?"

One can only guess. Dondero and Lennon—either or both—may have represented the Santa Cruz Electric. Possibly they were speculators thinking to turn a quick dollar. Swanton may have had private purposes or perhaps doubted the council's willingness to grant him a second franchise. That would explain the Smith petition. There may have been a falling out or misunderstanding between Swanton and Smith. In any case Swanton got his second franchise on April 17. Smith also got a franchise; it laid dormant for several months, then was declared forfeited.

Failing to halt or delay the Capitola Road in the Common Council, Logan and associates went to court to prevent it from operating in Pacific Avenue. An injunction was issued. On June 20, however, Judge Lucas F. Smith of Superior Court set it aside and denied Logan's petition. "Street railways have no proprietary interests in streets nor exclusive right to their use," Judge Smith ruled. "I am clearly of the opinion that Section 499 of the Civil Code . . . is not repealed and was not intended to be repealed by the statutes of 1901 or 1903. . . . The evidence shows that the franchise of the defendant is for the purpose of constructing a street railway out by way of the Odd Fellows Cemetery to the Powder Works, which unquestionably would be of great benefit to the public generally. The other company is willing to pay half for tracks and appurtenances, and has so offered. The only question remaining is to fix a fair value."

Logan and company appealed the ruling, arguing in part that the Powder Works issue was a red herring and the Capitola Road was not in earnest about building that branch. They got another temporary restraining order but this, too, was lifted July 17. Eight days later the appeal was denied, effectively slamming the door on further legal action.

The Santa Cruz Electric also pursued its final strategy: improving service. Work began in May to restore the old beachfront line from the bathhouses to the river, using 40-pound rail. The footbridge to East Cliff was rebuilt and a dance platform installed near the railroad bridge. A switch was put in allowing 10-minute headway to and from the beach. The first cars ran to the river on June 25, the company again appealing to the public to help expedite the service: "The cars of the Santa Cruz Electric Railway have been in the habit, during the winter months when the travel was somewhat light, for the accommodation of patrons, to stop at any and all points where people wished to get on or off, but as travel has materially increased, and as we are attempting to operate the river branch of the road we are compelled, in order that we may run the cars on anywhere near schedule time, to request the public to take and leave cars at street crossings only."

That fall the company restored full service to its Riverside Avenue branch. By year's end it boasted eight miles of track on "smooth and easy roadbed." Eighteen people were on the payroll. Cars ran every 15 minutes through the Lower Plaza to Vue de l'eau and the beach, alternating down Pacific Avenue and the Riverside Avenue branch.

Improvements continued into 1904. Two new cars were bought. The Walnut Avenue branch was renovated; new wire was strung, and the roadbed was raised and reballasted. On June 24, 1904, the first passenger car in five years passed over this branch—"which," noted the Surf, "is to be a regular thing. A new car has been put on, which will go from the beach by the way of Riverside Avenue extension and the river up Walnut Avenue to the Bedell."

RACING EASTWARD toward the Casino, Santa Cruz Electric No. 6 passes Capitola electric No. 13 at the Sea Beach Hotel.
Randolph Brandt Collection

PACKED FROM END TO END, No. 9 passes East Twin Lakes en route to Capitola. The event benefitted the "Library Furnishing Fund" and featured "Lady Conductors" during Free Library Day, December 29, 1903. *Charles Smallwood Collection*

7. Building the Capitola Road

THE CAPITOLA road was now (June 1904) operational from the beach to the Lower Plaza and, by way of Twin Lakes, to the Opal cliffs overlooking Capitola. Work was well under way at Capitola and commencing on the Arana Gulch branch, which had to be completed by October 15 under terms of a franchise granted July 24, 1903. The orange-yellow cars of the Capitola road now shared rails in Pacific Avenue with the blue cars of the Santa Cruz Electric. Competition was fierce on the beach run, the Capitola road maintaining half-hour headway and the Santa Cruz Electric 15 minutes.

All Santa Cruz had enthusiastically followed the building of the new electric.

Cars had begun arriving from St. Louis in April 1903, each equipped with two 40-hp motors. Nelson Mosher of the Loma Prieta Lumber Company, on Cedar Street, got the contract to remodel Ely's old carhouse into a modern 10-car barn. Track laying began that month. By May 1 rails were in place in Center Street, curving into Lincoln. A diamond switch was laid in Center Street op-

posite Calvary Episcopal Church (later removed because of protests by the rector and vestrymen). On May 30 rails of the Capitola road crossed those of the Santa Cruz Electric in Pacific from Lincoln to Soquel Avenue. Ties and track of the older company were removed and relaid. The work took all day, during which "blue line" service to the beach was suspended.

On June 10—the day on which, incidentally, the first electric car ran on the Monterey and Pacific Grove railway—a Capitola car tried the Lincoln-Soquel crossing, jumping the track because of an improperly made frog.

Two days later, track laying was reported near completion on the Twin Lakes line and at the beach, where the esplanade was widened from 35 to 50 feet to allow for a 15-foot separation between the Southern Pacific and Capitola electric. This was demanded by the Southern Pacific; the company and city complied. The *Sentinel* that day attacked sentiments against running the electric out 70-foot-wide Soquel Avenue, reminiscing about crowded Washington Street, Boston, where "we have seen car jams . . . often half a mile long. When will

Soquel Avenue be thus jammed? Not till the trees of the Big Basin have disappeared, and Santa Cruz is part of greater San Francisco."

By June 20 the company had eight cars ready to go: two open bench cars, five combinations, and a parlor car. Corrected by now was an earlier problem: undersize trucks that had to be replaced. On June 25 the first car made its way from Soquel and Pacific Avenues down Center Street to the beach, Supervisor W.E. Miller having the distinction of paying the first fare. On Saturday afternoon June 27, the cars began running from Twin Lakes to the beach, reportedly doing a good business. Regular service commenced the following day.

Attention now turned to Pacific Avenue. While still enjoined from operating cars on this street, the company sent in workmen July 11 to build a switch and connecting track in the Lower Plaza from Pacific Avenue to Front Street. The restraining order was lifted at 4:30 P.M. July 17. The first Capitola car went up the avenue at 5:45.

Tempers flared as rival crews jockeyed for position and patrons. On July 23 came a memorable event: the first (and fortunately only) recorded collision between cars of competing streetcar companies in Pacific Avenue. The plan was to maintain at least a five-minute separation between cars, but in this case, a Santa Cruz Electric car was following close on the rear fender of a Capitola car. The latter stopped suddenly, the Santa Cruz car ramming into it. The front end of the Santa Cruz car was caved in; nobody was hurt.

More cars were added. Ties and rails were laid along Water Street to the upper bridge for the Water-Ocean extension (this line was never finished). The company also asked permission to build a spur track in the esplanade, violating its charter, to improve the frequency of service. "The ruction between the civil authority and the Capitola electric railway at one time threatened to be serious and permanent," the *Surf* later explained, "but the judicious use of 'soft words' by W.R. Porter, the treasurer of the company, finally resulted in a better understanding, and the spur track on the esplanade, and a switch in Lincoln Street, will be laid by consent."

Work was meanwhile proceeding swiftly on the Twin Lakes-Opal extension. From what is now East Cliff Drive near Seventh Avenue, the track crossed the beach sands on a fill to the far embankment and climbed the cliff, turning northward along Brighton Avenue (now Twelfth Avenue) and then eastward along the present Cliff Drive to Lilydale (Seventeenth Avenue). At Seventeenth the car line became a narrow cut on a downgrade to a curve and station at Corcoran's Lagoon. At 26th Avenue the tracks again paralleled the Cliff Drive, running out to Opal (about 2,500 feet short of Capitola). Most of this distance was over private right of way—what is now Portola Drive.

The first trip to Opal came Saturday evening July 25 with Superintendent E.A. Cole at the controller and several guests, including Cole's family, Fred Swanton, Chief Engineer Murphy, and the *Surf's* editor, aboard the car—whose number was 13. Reported the *Surf:*

"Saturday evening a cat of Ethiopian color dashed across the track of the Santa Cruz, Capitola and Watsonville Railway, just as car No. 13 was moving out of the car barn to make its first run on the road, the first car to traverse the track from Santa Maria del Mar to Opal, near Capitola.

"Here is the prelude and the ground work of a good story of ill luck and cat-astrophe. But nothing happened to the cat or the car. The cat is still enjoying one of her 'nine lives' unharmed, and car No. 13 is carrying people in comfort and safety, and the new road is running all right, despite the omens, which are about the silliest survivals of the ages of superstition."

(LEFT) CLIMBING THE GRADE from Wood's Lagoon, car No. 9 approaches Atlantic Avenue. (RIGHT) Twin Lakes streetcar depot remained in service for more than two decades.
Both: Randolph Brandt Collection

Past Corcoran's Lagoon went the car, then:

"Presto! Up against a fence. From Del Mar to Capitola, the line runs through private property 'across the lots,' so to speak. The cattle guards had not yet been placed, and the thrifty farmers along the line had stretched temporary fences across the track between fields, so that the balance of the trip was diversified with frequent stops to indulge in the rural pastime of letting down the bars. This incident was a forcible reminder of the invasion of electric life into the most isolated and somnolent sections. Electric railways will soon pass nearly every schoolhouse, and with electric lights and telephones, be among the appurtenances of every farmhouse.

"The present terminus is at Opal on the bluff overlooking Capitola. A rustic path on the crest of the ridge between the steam railroad track and the cliff, leads down to Capitola. (No extra fare is charged for this exhilarating part of the trip.) Arrangements with the Southern Pacific Company have been made whereby the track of the steam railroad is to be carried northward, and the electric road will ultimately occupy the present track line of the steam road, and thus descend the grade into Capitola."

The editor was lavish in his praise of the car:

"Number 13 is one of the combination cars, built on the most approved models for electric railways. They are finished in cherry, ash and curly maple; will seat 36 in comfort, and carry as many more. By ingenious devices, the windows can all be dropped out of sight and sound, and the entire car made open. Curtains also make it possible to entirely close the car, and with curtains down and brilliant lights, the occupants of an evening may be made as cozy as if in a parlor. The center aisle is wider than in the older built cars, and the conductor's pedals are not likely to collide with those of passengers."

Regular service began July 26, with running times from Opal of about 15 minutes to the carbarn, 30 minutes to the corner of Soquel and Pacific, and 45 minutes to the Santa Cruz beachfront. The cars were said to be well patronized. Electric lights and a telephone were installed at Opal; the pathway to Capitola was improved. Free bus service was arranged to and from Camp Capitola, meeting all cars.

Trailers were introduced September 4. In October the company announced its purchase of a tract in Seabright fronting 150 feet on Railroad Street and adjoining the Southern Pacific track, where a new carbarn would be built replacing the antiquated structure on Soquel Avenue.

Excursions to Opal were an innovation. The first was on August 5: "Fresno Night" at Capitola. "The immense crowd was well handled although the cars were crowded to their utmost capacity," reported the *Surf.* "The Raisin City band left on the seven o'clock car and played as the car went through the streets. . . . The return trip by moonlight was a delightful one."

One of the highlight events that first year was "Free Library Day," a brainchild of the Capitola road's management. On this day—December 29, 1903—the company turned over the bulk of its receipts to a group of Santa Cruz women who were starting a fund to furnish the new public library. (It opened in mid-April 1904 on the same site as the present main library, built with a $20,000 gift from the Carnegie Fund on land provided

AN OLD HORSECAR BODY became a station on Atlantic Avenue above Wood's Lagoon.
UCSC, Preston Sawyer Collection

at modest cost by F.A. Hihn.) Recruited to collect fares that day was "a bevy of the prettiest young ladies of this city." Working only the "genteel" hours between 9 A.M. and 9:30 P.M., they donned natty conductors' caps, handled the bell ropes, and collected fares "like old trolley hands" on the beach and Opal runs. The receipts were $168 by one account and $144 by another.

Pearl Dalton, one of the conductors, remembered the day vividly. "We oogled all the money we could get out of our customers," she recalled with a laugh. "And we were very dressy." Frills, furbelows, and ruffles were worn along with the conductors' caps. At day's end Pearl produced the largest single amount: $22. All proceeds went to buy tables and chairs for the new library-to-be.

In January 1904 the company offices moved from the Hotaling Block to new quarters on Soquel Avenue outfitted also as a waiting room. A spur was completed to the Santa Cruz depot, and derailing switches were installed on both sides of the Southern Pacific track at the beach, requiring conductors to throw the switches before the electric cars could proceed. A switch was installed in the esplanade as allowed the previous August by the Common Council. And in May, work began to extend the road another 800 feet eastward along the beach. This extension, with a short spur at the end, was completed June 15.

On the Opal line, benches of the Capitola road along Soquel Avenue and Cayuga Street were painted red by the East Santa Cruz Improvement Association, as part of a community beautification project. Cattle guards were built by the company at road crossings in Del Mar. Switches were installed at Corcoran's, Del Mar, and in Soquel Avenue opposite the company's powerhouse, allowing 15-minute headway from the avenue to Opal. That service began May 24 to accommodate an Odd Fellows' picnic at Capitola. The round-trip fare to Opal was 25¢.

On March 8 Superintendent Cole attained a clear right-of-way from Opal to Capitola, after signing up the

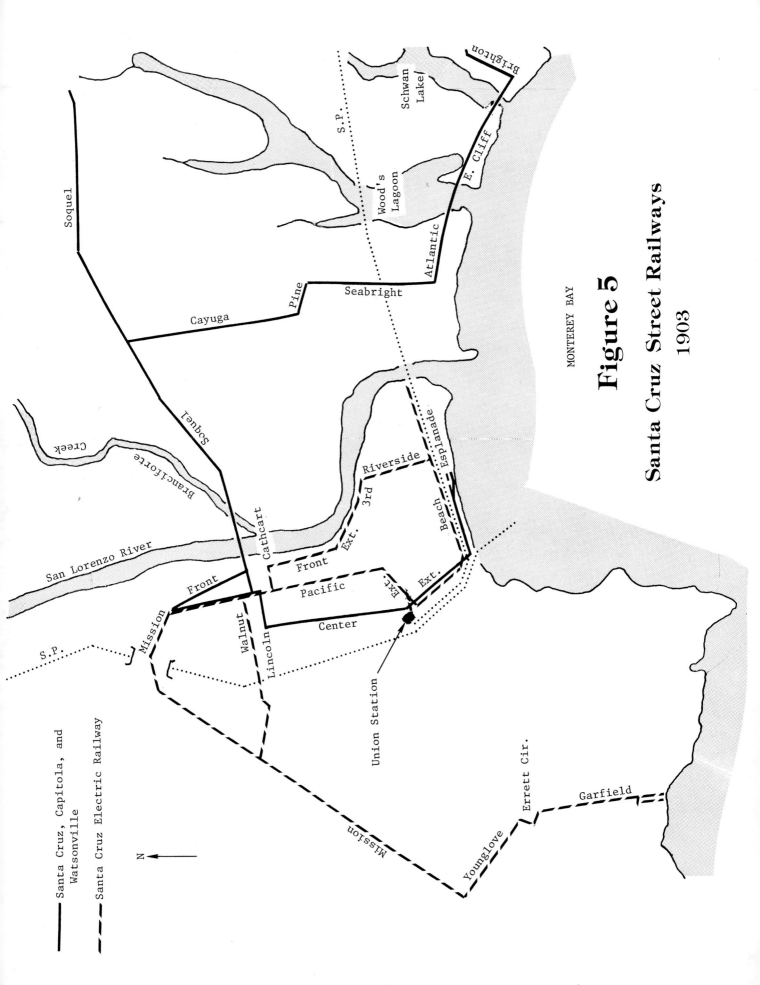

MONTEREY BAY

Figure 5

Santa Cruz Street Railways
1903

Santa Cruz, Capitola, and
Watsonville

Santa Cruz Electric Railway

Two Plus One at the Beach

FOR A TIME two streetcar operations plus Southern Pacific's big steam-powered trains ran along the beachfront.

(TOP) Capitola electric (SCC&W) car No. 11 heads west along the Santa Cruz beachfront, circa 1903.
Randolph Brandt Collection

(RIGHT) The track of the Capitola electric passed on the north side of the Casino buildings by September 1904, when No. 11 headed toward the magnificent pleasure palace.
Ayelott Photo, Randolph Brandt Collection

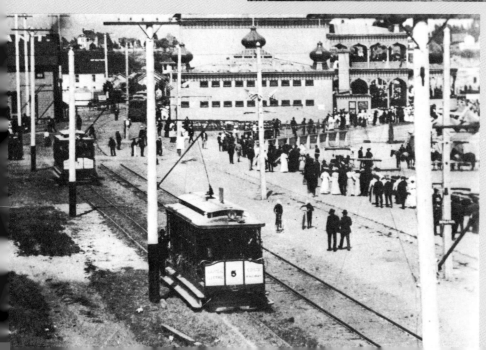

HEADING TOWARD DOWNTOWN, Santa Cruz Electric cars 5 and 7 run west from the Casino, along Beach Street. Capitola electric cars in the background are loading passengers. The two companies maintained spirited competition. *UCSC, Preston Sawyer Collection*

last property owner. "Work will be commenced at once," he declared, "as soon as the lumber, the Loma Prieta mill, the barn and other obstructions are removed." These were duly taken away. Yet to be removed, however, was a restaurant-saloon at the west end of the wagon bridge over the Soquel River at Capitola. The company intended to build a new span just south of this bridge, requiring the restaurant to be moved back several feet—all in all, a formidable engineering task.

By mid-April a steam shovel was positioned at Opal ready to begin cutting through the bluffs. Work went smoothly, the electric line departing from the Southern Pacific right-of-way near the latter's warehouse. Bridge construction began May 15; house movers using rollers had now commenced relocating the restaurant. The bridge pilings were in place by June 8 and, two weeks later, the span was finished except for the laying of rails. Crews were now working on the roadbed in Capitola.

The press of construction activity during the year had taken its toll of accidents, near misses, and the unfortunate death in Center Street of a seven-year-old boy run over by a construction car. That was in November 1903. Young Raymond Garelli, the son of Epifano Garelli, an Italian construction worker for the company, was returning from Laurel School with several companions when, for reasons unknown, he suddenly darted in front of the car. The wheels of the car and trailer passed over the lad. His lower limbs had to be amputated. The boy weakened after the operation and died the following day. The motorman and company were held blameless.

Several arms and legs were broken in various accidents. One workman suffered three broken fingers. Emil Shiller, engineer of the work train near Capitola, met with a freak accident in May 1904. A torpedo (a

TURNING INTO TREE-LINED 12th Avenue, Capitola electric No. 14 has just left Twin Lakes Trestle.
UCSC, Preston Sawyer Collection

percussion cap placed on rails as a warning device) unaccountably got mixed up with the coal in the tender and, when the fireman was shoveling coal, the torpedo fell and struck the track, exploding. A piece of shrapnel struck Shiller's arm, badly cutting it.

Car No. 10, loaded with passengers, experienced a close call. That was also in November 1903. The car was approaching the switch at Corcoran's where a large force of men was installing trolley wire. As related by the *Surf:* "One of the workmen was sent to turn the switch so as to permit the car to pass in safety, but the anxious workman . . . became so rattled that instead of closing the switch, threw it wide open. As the motorman had presumed the switch would be closed for him to pass, he was running along at a fair rate of speed, but upon seeing his danger, however, he at once applied the brakes, but he was too late. Off the track went the car into the sand with between 20 and 30 passengers on board.

"Motorman Morgareidge deserves great credit for the quick manner in which he brought the car to a stop. As it was, no one was injured and the passengers took the next car down and came on to the city. By the quick work of the men, the car was soon raised back on the track and running as usual, having sustained no damage to speak of."

Not all the dangers were from construction. On April 1, 1904, the company issued a stern warning about what it called a dangerous practice. "The attention of parents or guardians of several boys in Santa Cruz is called to the fact that these youngsters have devised velocipedes, fitting exactly the track of the Santa Cruz, Capitola and Watsonville Railway Company, and that they are making use of these tracks to run from Santa Cruz to Capitola. The company objects most strenuously to this practice, as it is liable to endanger any minute the life and limb of the boys engaged in this unlawful sport, and of passengers on their cars. It appears that the boys even cross trestles of the company and if a car should either meet or overtake them, some one or more would probably be injured."

THE TROLLEY TRACKS of the Santa Cruz, Capitola and Watsonville passed Lilydale at what is now 17th and Portola. *Harold Van Gorder Collection*

8. Granger Buys Santa Cruz Electric

THUS, IN June 1904, the two electric railways were mostly completed and locked in competition. The Santa Cruz Electric controlled the lucrative Vue de l'eau run and the best route—Pacific Avenue—to the beach, with branches to the San Lorenzo River and across town via Riverside and Walnut Avenues. The Capitola electric had its moneymaking line to East Santa Cruz, Twin Lakes, and Opal (finished almost to Capitola), a competitive but not as profitable route to the beach, and a very marginal branch to Arana Gulch. Neither company held a commanding advantage.

The value of the Santa Cruz Electric had been preserved. J. Philip Smith and associates were willing to await developments.

The Gardiner people had used the intervening months to consolidate their positions. In addition to spending $150,000 on the Capitola electric, they had electrified the Monterey and Pacific Grove and, in April 1904, announced ambitious plans to extend this road. McQuigg and R.C.P. Smith were officials of this company as well as the Capitola electric. O.Z. Hubbell had since died; his stock was voted by his widow Cora, and his position on the Capitola board of directors had been taken by Robert Goodnow. The syndicate had amalgamated its Monterey Gas and Electric Company with the Salinas Water, Light and Power Company to form the Monterey County Gas and Electric Company, with Gardiner as president and chief operating officer. Other acquisitions were being sought.

Swanton meanwhile had devised another big promotion: his Tent City development that gave the Santa Cruz beachfront its characteristic flavor of today. Plans were announced in August 1903 for a cottage and canvas community, with restaurant and family casino, to be built on and front the esplanade for a distance of several hundred feet. The project was blessed but not financially supported by the Southern Pacific, whose cooperation was vital. Public subscriptions were solicited in early October. The Santa Cruz Beach, Cottage, and Tent City Corporation was formed October 26 with Henry Willey, T.W. Kelly, Harley E. Irish, F.R. Walti, and George Staffler each pledging $4,000 and Swanton and H.F. Kron, $250 apiece. The prime movers, in addition to Swanton and Willey, were Kelly, a California native son and proprietor of a local store, and Irish, a native New Yorker, bank director, and local bookseller since the 1880s.

Part of the Tent City plan called for a new carriage and traction bridge across the San Lorenzo just below the railroad bridge, to be a joint project of the city, county, and Capitola electric with the Southern Pacific dedicating land for a street. This bridge if built would shorten by almost three miles the Capitola road's line to Seabright and Opal. The city and county approved in principle and the details were fixed: 410 feet of trestle approach with a 190-foot span, 13 feet for the streetcar tracks, 18 feet for the carriage roadway, a six-foot sidewalk, and an overhead crossing for the electric over the Southern Pacific. But costs killed the project.

Other parts of the plan progressed more or less on schedule. A storm in March 1904 caught the new casino unprepared; the outside studding was up but only lightly braced. Down it went, with damage estimated at a few hundred dollars. Another casualty of the storm was the old Dolphin bathhouse, now moved out onto the sand and used for storing chairs for the new casino. It, too, collapsed, its contents being strewn along the beach. Despite these adversities, the new casino and pleasure pier opened June 11. The Tent City dining room, at Beach and Cliff Streets, opened at noon five days later featuring a varied menu and array of special club breakfasts: No. 1 (10¢), coffee, tea or chocolate, rolls or toast, butter; No. 2 (20¢), two eggs plus the above; No. 3 (25¢), corned beef hash, with egg 5¢ extra; and so on up to No. 8 (65¢), fresh fruit in season, any kind of cereal with cream, two eggs any style, French fried potatoes, small sirloin steak, rolls and butter, coffee, tea or chocolate.

That same month—June 1904—brought a newcomer to the local transit scene, bent on resurrecting the old plan for a coastal electric railway from San Francisco through Santa Cruz to Monterey. This time the developers were in earnest and reportedly backed by abundant capital. Their local representative was none other than John Q. Packard, co-owner of the Big Creek Power Company and a man of substantial personal means. He applied to the county supervisors June 3 for a franchise from the city's west boundary to the county line, running between the county road and the seashore by an unspecified route. The supervisors granted this franchise three days later.

Rumors circulated. Some said the new interests would soon buy out both existing streetcar companies. Others thought the new company was just another front for the Gardiner people. In both cases the Santa Cruz Electric was seen as the target for a takeover, and it was—but from an unexpected source:

"F.S. Granger and family are going to Santa Cruz to reside," announced the *Surf* on June 22. "That's a brief statement in a San Jose paper. What it means, or may mean, to Santa Cruz, will be appreciated when it is understood that Mr. Granger is the man who promoted and financed, and constructed and recently sold the magnificent system of electric railways in Santa Clara Valley, extending from San Jose to the surrounding suburban towns. Mr. Granger is a robust man of powerful physique, active, energetic and forceful. It is not to be presumed that he is coming to Santa Cruz for his health, nor to indulge in sea bathing, or yet to linger by the beach and listen to the wild waves and the band concerts.

"Mr. Granger presumably has other business. At all events the *Surf* wishes to extend to him the glad hand, and to express the hope that he will become one of us.

"Hon. Wm. T. Jeter . . . of the Santa Cruz Electric Railway returned last evening from a business trip to San Francisco, where he was in conference with Mr. James Philip Smith of Paris, New York and Sunshine Villa, the principal owner of the road. Mr. F.S. Granger, Mr. J.W. Forgeus and others were also present. When interviewed concerning what transpired at this meeting, the parties are reticent. They decline to state that anything has happened. But the *Surf* has suspicions.

"The *Surf* has a suspicion that when the annual meeting of the Santa Cruz Electric Railway is held a new board of directors will be elected; that in due process of time it will develop that Mr. Smith has sold the road to Mr. Granger and the capitalists he represents, who put nearly a million dollars into the Santa Clara electric roads.

"The *Surf* suspects that in due time it will develop that Mr. Granger and associates have become the owners not only of the street railway, but other franchises in Santa Cruz. . . . The interurban roads built and equipped by Mr. Granger in the Santa Clara Valley are the finest west of the Rocky Mountains and not excelled in the United States."

The sale was confirmed the next day by the *Sentinel:*

"Papers were signed late Tuesday, June 21, between 'Silent Jim' Smith, principal stockholder in the Santa Cruz Electric Railway and F.S. Granger of San Jose, transferring to Mr. Granger a controlling interest in the road. The exchange was made Wednesday and the road is now in the hands of the San Jose man. No price was mentioned but it was learned upon good authority that it could only be spoken of in words expressing hundred thousands.

"The deal has been hanging fire for some weeks. Mr. Smith arrived at the Palace in San Francisco over a week ago, and since that time the deal was negotiated and closed up."

Interviews followed in both local newspapers in which Granger said he would assume control of the Santa Cruz Electric at once, put it in the best possible running shape, and perfect plans for extensions and tributaries. The roadbed will be improved, he said; the cars will be overhauled until they "resemble real streetcars." He discussed cooperation with the Capitola road and the possibility of 10-minute service in Pacific Avenue. "You know what has been accomplished in San Jose in a year," he declared.

Granger opened an office in the County Bank Building and, on June 28, took over temporarily as general manager of the Santa Cruz Electric. He, Jeter, and Irish were added to the board. West was named secretary. Regular elections were still a month away.

On July 5 Granger asked the Common Council for rights to operate from Front Street along Soquel Avenue and Ocean Street to the city limits and also, from the county supervisors, a franchise along Soquel, Ocean, and Branciforte Avenue to the Powder Mill. Both petitions were granted. He began reballasting the Vue de l'eau line, installing new ties and raising the track. Plans were announced for rebuilding the Vue de l'eau casino. And on July 19 he introduced a new car that startled the population along Pacific Avenue, as reported by the *Sentinel:*

"A streak of red, a flash of green, a trail of yellow, a clanging gong. This is not a resume of the fundamental elements of a Chinese joss house or the main ingredients of an oriental nightmare; it's merely a description of Car No. 10, which made its debut on Pacific Avenue Tuesday. The avenue has not yet recovered. As the car moved up the street, a hushed, awed silence fell over the thoroughfare. The Nile green trucks exercised an influence balefully fascinating.

"The frost-bitten hue of the trimmings growled hoarsely at the dead red that supports it, while the penetrating Celtic green that decks the axles is in violent altercation with the entire color scheme. Unless artist Will Lemos encounters the car without warning, no casualties are expected. At any rate we will stifle our aesthetic sense for the sake of the ten-minute service."

If Granger's intended cooperation with the Capitola road was achieved at the management level, not always so at the operator level, as evidenced by this report in the *Sentinel:* "Because of a difference of opinion as to which car had the right of way on Pacific Avenue Tuesday afternoon, Car No. 18 of the Capitola line and Car No. 3 of the Santa Cruz company attempted the always interesting feat of trying to go both ways at once over the same track. When it was obvious that neither conductor would give in, both cars stopped and stood facing each other on Pacific Avenue at Locust Street. After eloquent orations on the subject from both conductors, the Capitola car turned its trolley and started on its return route, leaving the way clear."

Santa Cruz cars 3 and 4 collided one afternoon opposite Blackburn Terrace, extensively damaging both cars and knocking their controllers out of gear. That snarled traffic for some time.

Despite these minor mishaps, the transition in management came about smoothly. Charles Chadwick, a friend of Granger's, replaced West as superintendent of the "blue line." Tranquility reigned. The only hint of possible further developments was a report of lengthy meetings between Granger and Warren Porter, treasurer of the Capitola road. In late July an informant—a "heavy stockholder in one of the companies"—told the *Sentinel,* "There is 'something doing' between the two roads. It may result in only a universal transfer service or it may result in a merging of the two roads. I think the last is very probable."

AFTER AMALGAMATION with Santa Cruz Electric, Capitola electric car No. 14 now uses the northernmost track along the beachfront, formerly used exclusively by Santa Cruz Electric. View is at Tent City.
Randolph Brandt Collection

9. Consolidation

SOMETHING WAS indeed "doing." On September 2 the *Union Traction Company* was quietly incorporated for 50 years and capital stock of $750,000 (7,500 shares) with $5,000 subscribed each by Cora E. Hubbell, R.C.P. Smith, and the company's seven directors: Warren Porter of Watsonville, McQuigg of Monterey, Granger of San Jose, and Forgeus, Willey, Jeter, and Gardiner of Santa Cruz. On September 18 the *Sentinel* predicted consolidation, with E.A. Cole to become general superintendent of the combined roads. However, formal announcement was withheld until October 4, the day that the first electric car entered Capitola to make its loop and return to Santa Cruz.

> "The Union Traction Company today absorbs the Santa Cruz Electric Railway and the Santa Cruz, Capitola and Watsonville Electric Railway," reported the *Surf* that day. "The directorate of the new company will be composed of M.V. McQuigg, J.M. Gardiner, W.R. Porter, and Henry Willey, from the Capitola company, and F.S. Granger, J.W. Forgeus, and Wm. T. Jeter, from the Santa Cruz Electric. The officers, as agreed upon, are Warren R. Porter, president; M.V. McQuigg, 1st vice president; J.W. Forgeus, secretary; and Henry Willey, treasurer. F.S. Granger will be the general manager for the system, and E.A. Cole superintendent.
>
> "The three directors named from the Santa Cruz company practically represent the entire stock of that company. The silent stockholders in the Capitola company are Mrs. Cora Hubbell, R.C.P. Smith, F.W. Swanton, and J.D. Schuyler.
>
> "We have no authority for so stating, but we do not believe it would be a bad guess to estimate the profits of the Capitola road this summer, running from Opal only, at $3,000 per month. We calculate that without curtailing the service—in fact, improving it—the economies of consolidation will give a credit balance to the unified system of $1000 per month over present income of the two roads operating as competitors."

The major change in service came October 29 when the orange-yellow cars of the Capitola road were taken off Pacific Avenue. Thereafter the corner of Soquel and Pacific became the exchange point between the Capitola cars, operating to the beach down Center

Street, and the Vue de l'eau cars, operating through the Lower Plaza and to the beach down Pacific Avenue. A thirty-minute headway was established to and from Capitola. Service was maintained on the crosstown branch from the San Lorenzo to the Bedell via Riverside and Walnut Avenues and, also, on the Arana Gulch branch. As of year's end the company reported 18 cars operating over 15 miles of main line (18 miles in all). Plans were announced for a new carbarn at Pacific Avenue and Sycamore Street to replace the aging Santa Cruz Electric barn on Pacific.

Granger had now severed his connection with Union Traction, for reasons unknown. A terse announcement November 27 said merely that he had sold out his railroad interests and did not want to remain in the corporation. He was then a defendant, with James W. Rea of San Jose, in a suit by a St. Louis man to recover $50,000 in alleged unpaid debts, a holdover from his Santa Clara railroading days. But this evidently was not a prime cause, because he showed up with Charles Chadwick in San Luis Obispo the following month promoting an electric line to Avila Beach and as late as 1907 in Hanford, California, on a similar adventure.

In any case, Granger resigned. His place on the Union Traction board was taken by Montroyd Sharpe. Final details of the merger were completed and, on January 20, 1905, the company authorized a bonded indebtedness of $750,000. At this meeting the major stockholder was the Santa Cruz, Capitola and Watsonville, voting 3,450 shares. Forgeus voted 2,200 shares and his real estate partner D.W. Johnston 500 shares. Also voting 500 shares apiece were Sharpe and James Normand. About $170,000 in 5% gold-coupon bonds was placed with the Pacific Mutual Life Insurance Company and the Anglo California Bank of San Francisco, largely through Forgeus' efforts. Another $80,000 was sold locally. The company reported assets of $1.07 million with receipts of $49,500 and operating expenses

of $32,000 during 1904, producing a net income of $17,500.

That same month—January 1905—the Norris and Rowe circus bought Vue de l'eau and six adjoining acres for its winter quarters, ending plans to restore the old casino. Two months later, on March 12, the railroad's trackage was attacked by a storm called the worst in 15 years. Washed away at Twin Lakes were 200 feet of pilings, bulkheads, and fill, halting service to Capitola and provoking an angry outburst from Mrs. Jacob Schwan, who had lived in the area many years and seen heavy storms roll huge waves against the coast there. She had warned Superintendent Cole not to put a fill at that

place, she told the *Sentinel*. To Cole she had said, "Who knows best? You or the Lord Almighty?" Now her prediction had come to pass. The fill was replaced with a trestle.

The company put some $70,000 into new cars and equipment during 1905 including a new powerhouse and carbarn at the foot of Pacific Avenue. At the same time, to reduce expenses, it halted service down Beach Street to the river, on the Riverside Avenue branch, and out to Arana Gulch. Walnut Avenue was cut back to a spur line operating only to Rincon Street (at the base of Weeks' Hill), and schedules were curtailed on Center Street except during the busy summer season.

Rumors began circulating in August that Henry Huntington was interested. Gardiner went to San Francisco in September for three-way talks with the Huntingtons and the developers of the new coastal electric road, now incorporated as the *Ocean Shore Railway Company*. Backing the latter, in addition to John Packard, were San Francisco financiers J. Downey Harvey, Walter Dean, C.C. Moore, and Alfred Bowen, whose name had been linked to the Petaluma and Santa Rosa electric road then under construction. The *San Francisco Call* reported a "master plan" whereby the Huntington interests hoped to consolidate all the coastal electric lines south of the Golden State:

> "A deal is being quietly effected between President Gardiner, of the Monterey Gas and Power Company, and Howard E. Huntington, son of the millionaire, for the purchase of the electric railway between Monterey and Pacific Grove, owned by the Gardiner syndicate. In fact, it is reported that the deal for the possession of the seven miles of road will be completed by the Hellmans, of this city, acting for the Huntingtons, in a few days.
>
> "Under the terms of the deal it is said that the Gardiner people will also turn over to the purchaser of their road the rights of way obtained a few weeks ago for an electric road from Monterey to Santa Cruz, by way of Salinas and Hollister, which, when built, will form an extension to the road between Monterey and Pacific Grove. It is common gossip that the Huntingtons and the owners of the proposed electric line between this city and Santa Cruz known as the Ocean Shore road, have an understanding whereby their interests will be harmonized so as to insure a through electric service from this city to Monterey and Pacific Grove.
>
> "President Gardiner . . . has been in San Francisco for several days in connection with the pending deal for his electric line."

The breakdown of these negotiations, coupled with later events, ended any reasonable hopes for a unified electric traction system along the shores of Monterey Bay. Expansion was over for the Monterey and Pacific Grove railway.

The collapse also signaled the withdrawal of Gardiner, McQuigg, and Cora Hubbell from Union Traction, their stock being acquired by Forgeus and possibly others. R.C.P. Smith and Montroyd Sharpe retained their holdings. That put Forgeus in charge of the company's negotiations, bringing into play his considerable contacts including John Martin of San Francisco, president of the California Gas and Construction Company, to whom Forgeus had recently sold the Watsonville Light and Power Company. Martin was known to be acquisition-minded; he had recently associated himself with a $650,000 traction development in San Jose and, with Eugene J. de Sabla, Jr., was now consolidating the multimillion-dollar Pacific Gas and Electric Company. Martin was to play an important role in future local developments.

It had been clear from the January 20 vote that the Gardiner syndicate still controlled Union Traction although Forgeus had an increasingly powerful voice. In March McQuigg, representing the Monterey County Gas and Electric Company, secured franchises to connect the Capitola and Monterey electric roads and also a contract—from the Monterey County Board of Supervisors—to build the Salinas extension on a 50-foot-wide right of way donated by the county, with a $50,000 bonus to be invested in rails. That opened the possibility that the Santa Cruz-Monterey connection might become a reality.

But the Gardiner people were anxious to sell.

THE OCEAN SHORE operated several steam locomotives, including No. 6 (above) on its isolated Santa Cruz segment, but never electrified its local trackage as it did a portion in San Francisco.
UCSC, Preston Sawyer Collection

10. Enter the Ocean Shore

DENIED Huntington's support, Downey Harvey and colleagues nonetheless decided to proceed with plans for a high-speed, double-track electric railway down the coast. Grading began simultaneously September 17 southwest of San Francisco and near the beach in Santa Cruz, where the June 1904 franchise called for scaling the bluff by a viaduct under Bay Street and a right of way along the general course of Major's Mill Creek to Delaware Street, thence out Delaware to the west city limits. This route resembled the old Bay and Coast (West Shore) franchise of earlier years.

The Southern Pacific promptly ran a spur track across the Ocean Shore's right of way down near the Santa Cruz wharves. Troubles mounted, doubtless precipitated by the Southern Pacific. Court actions by the Ocean Shore to rid itself of the spur and to force condemnation of a beachfront terminal site were denied. Despite all, the new road had completed a temporary Santa Cruz station by November 1 and laid six miles of track out Delaware Street toward the communities of Davenport and Swanton.

The Ocean Shore tried to buy Union Traction that fall, interested mostly in its power plant, franchises, and tracks to the river and to Capitola. Forgeus and company rejected that offer but, in January 1906, levied an assessment against capital stock to pay an outstanding indebtedness. "Seems to indicate that another deal is in prospect," commented the *Surf.* It was.

On February 3 the *Surf* reported that an option had now been taken on Union Traction by the Ocean Shore, which was running one car daily over the unused Beach Street line to the river so as to maintain that franchise. Two days later came a formal announcement of purchase, Harvey declaring his intent to open an outlet to Watsonville by means of the Capitola branch. The purchase price was not revealed.

Ownership by the Ocean Shore proved to be of brief duration. Two payments were made to the Union Traction stockholders, but then came the San Francisco earthquake and fire of April 19. This immense tragedy quickly caused funding sources to dry up. The Ocean Shore stopped paying, and Union Traction reverted to Forgeus and company.

The coastal road struggled fitfully on, obtaining a depot site in Blackburn Terrace in December 1906 and a sweeping Santa Cruz franchise from the Common Council in September 1907. This charter—never used—would have allowed the Ocean Shore to run rails up Cedar Street from Bay to about Lincoln, curving over private lands across Pacific Avenue to Front Street, south to Laurel and, by private right of way, back to Cedar. It was bitterly opposed by adjacent property owners. Packard personally promoted these developments, encouraging local investors to buy the company's bonds. He admitted before his death (October 1908) that he had sunk $218,000 of his personal funds into the Ocean Shore.

The company tumbled into bankruptcy in 1909, from which it went into receivership the next year. Operations continued for another decade, but the track from Santa Cruz to Swanton was never electrified and a 26-mile gap from Swanton to Tunitas (southern end of the San Francisco branch) was never closed. The Ocean Shore died a slow death, finally succumbing in 1920.

11. Earthquake and Fire

THE MORNING was April 19, 1906, and the time, shortly after 5 A.M. Dawn was just touching the eastern sky, and Santa Cruz was slowly awakening. In one instant the day held promise of splendor. The next, it was caught in the crush of an 8.25-scale earthquake that broke full force along the nearby San Andreas fault east and north of the city, high in the Santa Cruz Mountains.

This was the famous San Francisco earthquake of 1906, which, coupled with fire, demolished that city and laid down a swath of destruction 20 to 40 miles wide, running 200 miles from Salinas in the south to Fort Bragg in the north. Many communities within that belt were leveled. Santa Cruz, outside the zone of greatest fury, suffered only moderate damage.

The city experienced its first major temblor at 5:07 A.M. That drove many people into the streets. Then came two more temblors within eight minutes. A great roar was heard. Clouds of dust filled the air. Down went the courthouse. The northeast corner of the new, stone City Bank Building broke loose from its retaining walls. Down came parts of the stone, brick, and wood Farmers' Union Building, a section of its south wall smashing through the Unique Theater and another through the Lay Building on Soquel Avenue. The Hihn Block was damaged, as were the Methodist and Con-

JUST TWO MONTHS after being hit by the 1906 San Francisco earthquake, Santa Cruz had its own disaster, when Neptune Casino, brainchild of Fred Swanton, burned to the sand only two years after it was built. Undaunted, Swanton rented a circus tent and put up a makeshift casino for the summer season. Then, with help from John Martin and others, he rebuilt the casino, bigger and grander than ever! *UCSC, Preston Sawyer Collection*

gregational churches. Holes opened in the esplanade and in Front Street near Soquel Avenue. Water mains broke and twisted. Wires came down in some places. The city found itself crippled but able to function. Fortunately there was no fire either here or in Capitola, which likewise reported modest damage.

Seven or eight minor shocks were felt over the next couple of hours, during which the damage assessment continued. Nine persons died in a landslide near the Loma Prieta lumber mill, but no deaths were reported locally. Miraculously, even personal injuries seemed few in number.

The streetcar company considered itself lucky. Damage was limited to some bent and twisted rails, distressed roadbed, and the collapse of one wall at the Pacific Avenue carbarn. All the rolling stock escaped injury, even two cars abandoned in the shadow of the City Bank and IOOF Building by their frightened crews.

Company workmen and cars helped remove debris

from the city streets, just as they had after the great fire of 1894. Trolley wires were restrung, rails and roadbed relaid, and service restored soon to all branches.

No sooner had the city dug out from the earthquake when it suffered its second great disaster of 1906—the spectacular June 22 blaze that destroyed Fred Swanton's two-year-old Neptune casino. Fireman arrived to find "Swanton's Castle," as it was called, enveloped in flames. When the fire died down, all that remained of a $204,000 investment were the hot baths, parts of the electric pier, and a portion of Tent City. Swanton, out of town on one of his frequent "booster trips," returned to find the property in ruins.

Local officials put the loss at $100,000. Swanton himself estimated $67,000 as against $64,000 in insurance. Assets of the Tent City corporation were said to be $40,000 versus $87,000 in liabilities. The corporation was now down and out, he declared. What happened next was possibly his greatest promotion.

John Martin was in town investigating acquisitions for Pacific Gas and Electric Company. Even before the casino's ashes were cold, so the story goes, Swanton took Martin to the top of Beach Hill, laid out a half-million-dollar rebuilding program, and persuaded the San Franciscan to invest heavily. Both Martin and de Sabla pledged large amounts. Final arrangements probably were made at that time for their purchase of the Santa Cruz Electric Light and Gas Company and the Co-operative Electric Light Company, promptly consolidated into the Coast Counties Power Company. The discussions may have been many-sided, involving Forgeus, Packard, and perhaps even Downey Harvey, who was well acquainted with Martin and de Sabla through power company dealings. What transpired in any case were overtures by Martin and de Sabla to buy both Union Traction and the Big Creek Power Company.

Moving quickly, Swanton secured from the Common Council a 50-year lease on properties fronting the beach, overcoming opposition by the Hihn real estate company. Then he consolidated several local enterprises and formed a new company to rebuild the casino and plunge baths on a "greater and grander scale than before." Meanwhile, aided by temporary facilities, he reopened the plunge baths July 6 and then the entire amusement park. In September, delegates to the Republican state convention gathered at the beach under a large canvas tent to choose a successor to Governor Pardee.

Incorporated as the Santa Cruz Beach Company, Swanton and his partners reportedly spent $750,000 for a larger casino, natatorium, and extended boardwalk, all of which opened to the public—with appropriate fanfare—on June 15, 1907. The Moorish-styled structures, described by the *Surf* as "the pride of the Pacific Coast," corresponded in length "with the famous ferry building facing the bay of San Francisco." Swanton is said to have employed 500 men at $1,500 a day building them. He brought Michael Angelo Garibaldi from Italy to make statuary and copies of the masters, which were placed in the natatorium and on the roof of the casino.

The casino contained six private dining rooms, a grill room, and a bar modeled after the Waldorf-Astoria's. Upstairs was a combination dancing pavilion, convention hall, and theater that brought opera stars and other famous personalities to Santa Cruz. Swimmers in the natatorium, or plunge, were sheltered by a steel and glass canopy. The buildings were lavishly illuminated for night entertainment and protected by fire sprinklers with an auxiliary water pipe out into the bay.

To promote his new venture, Swanton distributed pamphlets from Los Angeles to Tonopah extolling the virtues and beauties of Santa Cruz. Brass bands paraded along the boardwalk, and fireworks lit the night skies. Pleasure seekers came by the thousands. For the more sophisticated, according to one account, Swanton anchored the pleasure ship Balboa in the bay just beyond the reach of the law, offering gambling, the company of "shady ladies," and other enticements to the visiting tourists.

In 1910, flushed by success, Swanton reportedly spent $550,000 building the Casa del Rey Hotel across from the casino. John McLaren, the noted architect of San Francisco's Golden Gate Park, was hired to design the gardens around the hotel. The huge expense and a national depression helped cause the Santa Cruz Beach Company to fail in 1912. Swanton was forced into bankruptcy.

Undaunted, he helped organize the 1915 Panama-Pacific Exposition in San Francisco. A chrome mine near Placerville the following year helped to recoup his finances but did not prove to be the bonanza he hoped. He returned to Santa Cruz, serving as its mayor from 1927 to 1933. Once again bankrupt, he listed his income as $100 per month. Swanton's final years were those of privation: continuing aspirations but very little success. He died almost penniless in September 1940, barely able to pay his own funeral expenses.

12. Martin Buys Union Traction

"**M**ARTIN BUYS Union Traction," declared the *Sentinel* Sunday morning July 8, 1906. "On Saturday afternoon at about five o'clock, a deal of great importance to this city was consummated, whereby the Union Traction Company disposed of its entire interests to the Coast Counties Power Company, of which John Martin and Eugene de Sabla are the leading owners. The consideration paid is not made public." The *Sentinel* continued:

"The transfer has been only about two weeks in incubation. The new owners intend to make several extensions and to spend a large amount of money at once. The present track will also be improved. The part of it between the end of Mission Street and Vue de l'eau will be taken up and relaid with 50-pound rails.

"The deal reported above will be a genuine surprise to *Sentinel* readers, as it had been understood right along that the Ocean Shore railway interests were to be the purchasers of the local streetcar system. The deal with the Ocean Shore people fell through and only two weeks ago Messrs. Martin and de Sabla made overtures for the inclusion of the local company in their new Coast Counties Power Company, which is a holding company for their Santa Cruz County interests. They are reaching out after the Big Creek Power Company, the final transfer of this company into their hands having been delayed through the unwillingness of one of the stockholders to sell."

Union's stockholders at sale time were Warren Porter, Henry Willey, Montroyd Sharpe, G.H. Normand, D.W. Johnston, and Forgeus, who held controlling interest. The formal transfer to Martin and associates came on July 16. Willey and Forgeus kept small holdings and remained on the board. Joining them were Martin; his private secretary C.E. Mallock; R.H. Stirling, manager of the Watsonville Light and Power Company; and Van E. Britton, son of John A. Britton, president of Pacific Gas and Electric and a close personal friend of Martin. Young Britton became vice-president and Mallock secretary of Union Traction, Martin taking over as president. E.A. Cole was retained as superintendent. The company's business offices were moved from Santa Cruz to San Francisco.

Martin then discussed his plans for Union Traction. Schedules would not change, he said, and fares would remain the same. He hoped to extend the road in various directions, with lines radiating out to Big Trees six miles north and to Soquel five miles east, making a loop with the company's Capitola branch. The long-talked-of extension to Watsonville was not beyond the realm of possibility.

Forgeus was locally hailed during the next few weeks as the generator of many recent industrial and real estate improvements including development of the 8,000-acre San Vincente land grant and resurgence of the Santa Cruz Lime Company, now a thriving producer of lime rock and timber. But most of the atten-

JOHN MARTIN, co-founder of Pacific Gas and Electric Company. In 1906 he bought Union Traction, double-tracked and standard-gauged the railway system (1907), and built the Laveaga Park branch (1908 and 1910).
Courtesy Pacific Gas and Electric Company

tion went to Martin, a man of "inexhaustible energy, an indomitable will to succeed, an alert and facile mind, and a powerful physique." Here was a man of humble origin who through his own efforts had risen to great wealth and prestige, whose preoccupation was fashioning a net of utility and traction companies spanning Northern California. The local newspapers reported highlights of his career.

Born 1858 in Indianapolis, he had spent his boyhood in Brooklyn and, since age 13, had fended for himself. Real estate experience in Alabama and employment by the Armours in Chicago preceded his arrival in California in 1891. In San Francisco he became a bookkeeper for Husband and Brooks, waterfront coal dealers who subsequently declared bankruptcy. He then worked as a drummer for the U.S. Cast Iron Pipe Company, establishing his own business—John Martin Company—to sell pipe and pig iron.

Among Martin's acquaintances was an electrician who held a letter from the Stanley Electrical Manufacturing Company of Pittsfield, Massachusetts, authorizing him to sell its products on a commission basis. Martin apparently discussed with him the merits of electric power and Stanley equipment. Another of Martin's acquaintances, the manager of a Bay Area drugstore and owner of a mine in the Mother Lode country, was also interested in electric power. He in turn knew a young man, Eugene de Sabla, who with others was developing a powerhouse in Nevada County on the South Yuba River, above Grass Valley. Thinking to help Martin to a pipe contract, the friend arranged a luncheon meeting with de Sabla in San Francisco in 1894. Martin reportedly was late for the meeting, explaining when he arrived that the delay was occasioned by the birth of his fifth child that morning.

Charles M. Coleman, in his book *P.G. and E. of California,* reconstructs that meeting. The three men discussed power and pipe and electrical equipment. De Sabla told of studies of available generators, expressing his opinion that Stanley made the best generators for his Nevada County purposes. Martin seemed more interested in this phase of the discussion than in selling pipe. He and de Sabla did not meet again for two or three months, de Sabla assuming that Martin had forgotten their noontime discussion until one day he met Martin on Montgomery Street. "I'm ready now for your order," said Martin. "What order?" asked de Sabla. Then the story came out.

Intrigued by the talk of opportunities in electric power, Martin had gone to Pittsfield to meet William Stanley, the inventor and head of the manufacturing company. Although Martin had no training or experience in electrical construction, he was convincing enough to get the California agency for Stanley's products.

De Sabla did buy from Martin, commencing a long and mutually profitable association. The Nevada County project grew and prospered. Others soon followed: Sacramento Electric, Gas, and Railway; Yuba Electric Power; Butte County Power; California Central Gas and Electric. Martin sold equipment to these companies, but his enthusiasm gradually turned to utility company promotion. In just one five-month period he acquired 12 local utilities from Chico to Colusa. Most of the holdings were eventually consolidated into two companies: California Gas and Electric, and San Francisco Gas and Electric. Then he and de Sabla created a new corporation, Pacific Gas and Electric, to amalgamate these two companies. That was in October 1905. The new corporation took charge January 2, 1906, bringing scores of utilities under one management.

Beyond these were many separate properties in which the two men held large or controlling interests, often with backing from elsewhere. Coast Counties was one such. The local newspapers thought it was part of Pacific Gas and Electric but it wasn't, at least for many years to come. One of Martin's backers in Santa Cruz

was longtime associate John C. Coleman, a wealthy ex-miner from Grass Valley, of English extraction, who favored expansion of both Coast Counties and Union Traction.

A "SACRAMENTO" CAR on Mission Street, Sept. 22, 1907, with workmen installing a track switch. View is in front of Bedell House, between Otis and Taylor.
UCSC, Preston Sawyer Collection

13. Broad-Gauging the System

DURING THE SUMMER and early fall of 1906, Martin was preoccupied with rebuilding facilities of the Pacific Gas and Electric Company, which had been hard-hit by the April earthquake. The company was compelled to borrow $1.4 million over a nine-month period to complete the rebuilding.

That fall, however, he installed F.E. Fitzpatrick as general manager of Coast Counties and also, replacing Mallock, as secretary of Union Traction. Brought in as general manager and purchasing agent for the streetcar company was young S. Waldo Coleman, John's son and a graduate electrical engineer whose professional experience included a couple of years with General Electric in Schenectady, New York, and a brief stint with the Petaluma and Santa Rosa electric railway.

Martin unveiled ambitious plans for broad-gauging and double-tracking the system, expanding the Pacific Avenue carbarn, manufacturing his cars locally, and building several important new branches. At the beach, he said, he hoped to persuade the Southern Pacific to "go inside, with the electric double-tracked on the Bay side." He wanted to see the esplanade widened to 60 feet and ornamented with palms and flowers. He envisioned new lines running from Capitola to Soquel; from the city center to the IOOF cemetery and, by a different route, to de Laveaga Heights; and from the casino directly across the San Lorenzo River to the Seabright line, then to a junction with the proposed Capitola-Soquel branch. These new lines would add some 16 miles of track, he estimated, nearly doubling the present system.

TRACK CREWS WORKED Mission Street, then moved into Pacific Avenue to widen the track gauge. Narrow-gauge service was temporarily maintained down Center Street to the beach and out Soquel Avenue to Twin Lakes-Capitola, requiring this mixed-gauge crossover at Soquel and Pacific. Photo was taken in April 1907. *Harold Van Gorder Collection*

In December 1906 the company began soliciting support for standard gauge with double tracks on the heaviest traveled portions, especially Pacific Avenue. "The property owners along the avenue seem much in favor of a double track," Manager Coleman told the *Surf* on January 5. "Already a large majority of those owning property between Lincoln Street and the Plaza have signed the petition. . . . In the past, some have thought that the avenue was too narrow for two tracks. In other cities it is found that a double track in a narrow street, instead of congesting traffic, greatly relieves it. This is primarily caused by the fact that in a double track system, the cars on one track go only in one direction, thereby tending to keep the wagon traffic on the proper side of the street. With the double track standard gauge, as proposed, there will still be ample space between the outside rail and the curb for the largest vehicles."

Armed with community support, Martin approached the Common Council January 7 for blanket rights to a standard-gauge, double-track system using 60-pound rail. The council unanimously consented January 14 under a suspension of normal rules; the franchise forbid crossovers in Pacific Avenue from Lincoln to the Plaza, and the company agreed to foot all costs for setting back the sidewalks three feet on both sides of the avenue.

Surveyors entered Pacific Avenue February 20 preparing for the double-tracking. Charles F. Brower, contractor, began work a week later on a 40- by 150-foot addition to the carbarn. E.A. Cole resigned March 1 as superintendent, Albert S. McCormick replacing him temporarily as trainmaster. J.H. Gill was named roadmaster and George L. Fitzgerald master mechanic. Coleman took active charge of the company's day-by-day operations.

Union Traction filed amended articles of incorpora-

tion in March stipulating the proposed new branches. The system's total length, as envisioned, would be 34 miles. A schedule of priorities was established. First to be attacked would be Pacific Avenue and Mission Street, with beach service maintained down Center Street and Vue de l'eau service out the Walnut Avenue branch. Then the crews would complete the Vue de l'eau branch, the Capitola branch, the new North Santa Cruz line to de Laveaga Heights, and the new line from Capitola to Soquel. The delays between narrow- and standard-gauge service would be minimized to reduce public inconvenience.

In that month the company listed as its rolling stock 18 St. Louis motor cars and two trailers served by a 500-hp station plant. The motor cars had Taylor and Bemis trucks and were equipped with Westinghouse motors. Martin was president with L.P. Law vice-president and Henry Malloch secretary-treasurer. The authorized debt was still $750,000 in 5% gold-coupon bonds with $300,000 now issued and $450,000 held in treasury. San Francisco's Union Trust Company was now the mortgage trustee. Conditions stipulated that the treasury bonds could be issued for extensions and improvements at 75% of their face value but not unless net income was sufficient to pay the interest on all outstanding bonds.

In June 1907 the company cut its fares to Capitola from 15¢ one way—25¢ round trip—to a straight 10¢ per ride. This was followed in September by commutation books with a nickel fare to Capitola for a 60-coupon book or 6⅔¢ per ride for a 15-coupon book.

Construction began June 6 in Pacific Avenue, one block at a time. Temporary rails were laid in Center Street from Lincoln to Walnut, allowing materials to be transported from the main depot up Center and Walnut for retracking Mission Street. Five California-type cars were obtained from Martin's Sacramento Electric, Gas, and Railway subsidiary; one was on hand early in June, with the others reportedly en route.

Martin failed to reach agreement with the Southern Pacific about exchanging rights of way at the beach, so a single-track, standard-gauge line was built along the existing route. A heavy retaining wall was constructed against Beach Hill to protect the line west of the Sea Beach Hotel.

By August 30 the crews were about done in Mission Street and preparing to move to East Santa Cruz. Standard-gauge cars began running to the beach on September 13; patrons from Capitola and the east side were advised that day to transfer to the new cars at Pacific Avenue. The narrow-gauge track was then removed from the esplanade although left in Center and Lincoln Streets. The company built a small station on the Pacific Avenue extension to shelter passengers from the winter rains.

September 25 marked the inauguration of standard-gauge service to Vue de l'eau. Fifteen-minute service was maintained at first because of a lack of cars but reduced to 10 minutes in mid-October when new

rary car shed was built at Del Mar for protecting and repairing the narrow-gauge equipment. Broad-gauge service opened to Capitola on November 14. Eventually the narrow-gauge cars were scrapped or otherwise disposed of, and the shed was torn down.

As regards the North Santa Cruz branch, the Common Council on August 5 gave Martin a franchise from the Lower Plaza out Water Street to Morrissey Avenue, up Morrissey to Fairmount Avenue, and across private lands to de Laveaga Heights. Terms called for suitable fenders on all cars and 2% of the gross proceeds to the city treasury. Construction was to begin within four months and be completed within three years.

Another stipulation was for Union Traction to build its own streetcar bridge across the San Lorenzo at Water Street just south of the existing wagon bridge (upper bridge). Martin agreed and submitted his bridge plans to the council; approval came September 3, and grading began at once. By early October piles were being driven for the bridge. The iron and concrete work got under way the following month, as did assembly of the steel spans. Company crews began driving piles in

TROLLEY STATION built in 1907 on Pacific Avenue extension near Union Station.
Randolph Brandt Collection

equipment was added: four St. Louis cars, a couple of combinations, a company rebuilt, and two single-track Hammonds. The company installed a switch at Bellevue Avenue early in December, cutting the running time on a round trip to Vue de l'eau from 60 to 48 minutes.

Work was meanwhile progressing on the Capitola branch. In mid-June the county supervisors granted their own comprehensive standard-gauge franchise covering this line. That same month a new streetcar bridge was opened over Wood's Lagoon. Previously the cars had used temporary rails on the adjoining public wagon bridge.

Crews moved into Cayuga Street and Seabright Avenue in early September. Work began on strengthening the Capitola bridge and also the Soquel Avenue trestle alongside the covered bridge. By mid-month Soquel Avenue was torn up from the trestle to Cayuga. Broad-gauge cars began operating along Soquel in early October from Pacific to Cayuga, where patrons transferred by bus to Seabright and boarded narrow-gauge cars to Twin Lakes, Del Mar, and Capitola. A tempo-

December for the Water Street crossing of Branciforte Creek. No track had been laid by year's end, but all was in readiness to finish the line.

The construction itself produced no accidents this time, but misfortune seemed to dog the company starting September 10 with the electrocution of Manuel Raeisento, a 40-year-old Portuguese workman who touched a live wire in the transformer room at the carbarn. John Todd was injured September 12 while trying unsuccessfully to board a moving car. Nick Rooney was run over that same day by another car; his leg was amputated September 13. On September 17, J.P. Drake, a company employee, was struck by a trolley and swept off the top of a repair car, breaking his arm in two places.

The toll mounted. On October 6 a conductor named Hadley was dragged by a Union Traction car near the Ocean Shore crossing, suffering sprains and bruises; he was off work for a week. Fred Beecher, working on the Water Street traction bridge, severely cut his foot with an adz. Early in November a boy fell off this bridge, fortunately landing in sand and escaping serious injury.

HEADING BEACHWARD, "Sacramento" car No. 4 is southbound on Pacific Avenue between Cooper and Water Streets.
Vernon J. Sappers Historical Collection

Also, pushing the limits of probability, two unrelated accidents involving streetcars happened at the same location on the same day. The site was Mission Hill and the date, October 21. The first was a runaway car that got away from its motorman because of faulty brakes and slippery track. It careened down the hill, its front trucks following the rails but its rear trucks jumping the track. It hit a pole in front of Orchard's candy store, causing no injuries but badly frightening the passengers. The second was a three-way mixup involving a streetcar, heavily loaded wagon, and light rubber-tired buggy. Down the hill came the wagon, full of granite from a demolished building. Right behind it came the streetcar, which struck the wagon and shoved it into the buggy, which collapsed. The drivers of the wagon and buggy were slightly injured.

There were lighter moments. One day on the Seabright line, a very pretty girl—one of the prettiest in the east suburbs, claimed the *Surf*—got her three hatpins caught in the uniform and buttons of a young conductor while leaving a streetcar. Cheered on by the other patrons, the two wiggled and squirmed around trying to disengage themselves. Finally free, the girl disembarked, waving gaily at those aboard. The conductor, a bachelor, allowed as how he would like to meet that girl again.

Generally speaking, the public seemed pleased with Union Traction. Edwin Yantis warmly remembered those times. As he told the *Sentinel's* Margaret Koch in April 1965, he had come to Santa Cruz in 1907 and gotten a job right away as a conductor. Each car was operated by two men: a motorman and a conductor. Each accommodated 30 passengers except when others squeezed in. "It cost 10¢ to go to Capitola," he recalled. "But even with only collecting nickels, we would take in from $80 to $100 a day."

In summertime the company operated 15 cars. They ran to Capitola every quarter hour. In winter they ran every half hour. "Double shift in summer," Yantis remembered. "Had about 60 men working then."

He got up at 5 A.M. and walked two miles to reach the Pacific Avenue carbarn by 6 A.M. "All runs started there at 6 A.M.," he said, recalling that one of the most important tasks each morning was transporting students to Santa Cruz High School from as far away as Capitola.

AT THE SOUTHERN PACIFIC crossing at Seabright Avenue, car No. 14 pauses for customers. Behind the S.P. station (left) is the Seabright Hotel. *Randolph Brandt Collection*

S. WALDO COLEMAN, General Manager of Union Traction since 1906, became President of Coast Counties Power Company AND Union Traction in 1912, replacing John Martin. *Blank-Stoller Photo, Courtesy Lewis V. Coleman*

14. Coleman Takes Charge

BY YEAR'S END 1907 both companies—Coast Counties and Union Traction—were doing well. Daily gas sales were up to 120,000 cubic feet, a 50% increase over 1906. There were 563 new gas customers and 654 new electrical customers. The utility installed 242 horsepower more generating capacity during 1906.

Financial returns from Union Traction were also said to be good and on the upswing. The physical value of the company's properties and equipment was put at more than $600,000. It seemed reasonable that the proposed extensions might be built: from Capitola to Soquel, out Ocean Street to the IOOF cemetery, and perhaps even to Big Trees (the *Surf* had once considered this branch a foregone certainty). But such was not the case. Unusual circumstances had put heavy personal financial pressure on Martin. Also, an Eastern money crisis had sent financial shock waves through the nation, drying up the sources of capital. Union Traction's era of expansion was nearing an end.

Martin had run into stormy financial weather. In addition to the $1.4 million borrowed by Pacific Gas and Electric to rebuild following the earthquake, the company faced nearly $1 million in bond interest due July 1, 1907. One way out was bankruptcy, allowing the company to fall into receivership. Martin, de Sabla, and the other directors opposed this and pursued another plan reported September 12 by the *Surf:* "The assessment of $10 a share on the stock of the Pacific Gas and Electric Company, which became delinquent on August 31, has resulted in an unusual transaction in the securities of that company. The entire issue of common stock, amounting to $20 million, has been turned back into the treasury of the company, while the assessment on the preferred stock has been paid in full, amounting to a total increase in the company's resources of $1 million. The issue of 20 million of common stock has been held by the banking firm of Halsey and Company." The article went on to report unfounded rumors of an impending takeover of Pacific Gas and Electric by other interests, Martin and the bankers "maintaining a discreet silence."

By this maneuver Martin, de Sabla, and associates kept control of the giant utility, although at considerable personal cost. Martin had to come up with $200,000 to pay the assessment on his preferred stock. Pacific Gas and Electric weathered the storm, floated a bond issue, and was board-listed in 1910 by the New York Stock Exchange.

The second important problem was the Eastern monetary crisis, impelled by a bad market that plunged to a crash in October 1907. A run on banks began late that month which, despite a brief banking holiday, did not end until Christmas. Much money was withdrawn from circulation. The two circumstances led to a reassessment by Martin and colleagues of their Santa Cruz holdings, including a reevaluation of the growth potential. Bank deposits in the community had risen more than threefold (to $6 million), yet improvements were up only 50% (to $4.25 million) and personal property had climbed only $130,000 (to $1.57 million). What this meant was that gains in some sectors were offset by deterioration in others. It was not an encouraging pattern.

So the partners scrapped expansion plans for Union Traction except for the North Santa Cruz branch, which held promise of immediate return from real estate sales once the line was operating. In December they organized the Laveaga Realty Company to handle sales, appointing Netherton and Torchiana their corporate counsel and the Santa Cruz Investment Company their general agents. Henry Willey became president of Laveaga Realty with Martin first vice-president, Warren Porter second vice-president, H.A. Van C. Torchiana secretary, and Coleman treasurer. Coleman was named manager for all work connected with improving the property.

In April 1908 Martin declared his intent to proceed with the Laveaga Park branch, as it was now called, despite what he termed "the money stringency and uncertain commercial conditions." The Water Street

WHIZZING ALONG THE EDGE of Monterey Bay, a Santa Cruz-bound car heads westward across a trestle at Twin Lakes, on the Capitola Branch.
Randolph Brandt Collection

(LEFT) CAR NO. 18 IS WESTBOUND at Opal, on the Capitola branch.
Vernon J. Sappers Historical Collection

(BELOW) SEA BEACH HOTEL makes an impressive background for this view of Union Traction No. 5, circa 1908. The hotel was completely destroyed by fire in June 1912.
Randolph Brandt Collection

AFTER THE LOOP WAS REMOVED (ABOVE) Capitola cars used the Electric Station at Monterey and Capitola. Before it disappeared (below) a westbound car used the Capitola loop in standard-gauge days.   *Both: Randolph Brandt Collection*

Capitola Collage

LEAVING CAPITOLA-BY-THE-SEA, an electric car has just crossed the bridge. Note the profusion of automobiles along the Esplanade. *Randolph Brandt Collection*

ANOTHER VIEW of the Capitola bridge. Behind is the higher Southern Pacific railroad bridge. *Randolph Brandt Collection*

IT'S A FINE Spring day (below) as we see another trolley leaving Capitola. Behind is the beach and Monterey Bay.
Vernon J. Sappers Historical Collection

THE LAVEAGA PARK TERMINUS, looking back toward the city. Car No. 17 is seen approaching the park. Union Traction built a semaphore at the park entrance to call cars from the terminus at Martin Blvd. It soon became a target for mischief-makers.

Randolph Brandt Collection

TWO TRANSFERS (right) from Santa Cruz's electric railway era.

Stephen D. Maguire

bridge would be finished; in addition to more than $1 million already expended on Santa Cruz enterprises, he and his colleagues expected to spend much more. Coleman affirmed the plans in July, telling the *Sentinel:* "We are simply waiting for City Engineer Williams to complete his survey of the grade of the street and we will continue our track out as far as the junction of Morrissey Avenue and Fairmount Avenue, in the Laveaga Park tract, opening up all that inviting landscape to settlement as a close suburb of Santa Cruz."

Construction began August 17 in Water Street. On October 4 work cars passed over the new Water Street bridge, in which was mounted a plaque reading "1908—Union Traction Company. John Martin, President. F.E. Fitzpatrick, Secretary. S.W. Coleman, General Manager. W.M. Thomas, Engineer." Service commenced October 15 to the end of Morrissey Avenue and November 3 to Fairmount Avenue, where piles of sand and stacks of trolley poles awaited the continuation to Martin Boulevard. That work was soon finished, patrons transferring to a horsecar at Martin Boulevard that carried them up to the park via Pacheco Avenue and Prospect Heights.

On June 10, 1910, the Common Council approved a franchise for electrifying the Laveaga horsecar line. Through electric service was inaugurated to the park's main gate on July 2. A semaphore was erected near the gate to signal motormen to continue up to the park; otherwise, the cars terminated at Martin Boulevard.

A SPECIAL STUB TRACK was built for shuttle car No. 20 in front of the Casa del Rey Hotel. Note the "Casa del Rey" roofboard.

Randolph Brandt Collection

There were other changes. All cars were decked out in the Union Traction color scheme: battleship gray with red trim. In 1908 the company relocated its tracks in Pacific Avenue extension from the side to the center, laying sidewalks on both sides of the street. The next year rails were removed from Walnut Avenue, from Soquel Avenue beyond Cayuga Street, and from Center Street except for the spur to the railroad depot. (These abandonments were not formally approved until October 1911.) A short connection was built to the Southern Pacific yards, curving from Sycamore Street to enter the yards west of the carbarn. In 1911, at Swanton's request, the company built a short spur up Cliff Street to serve patrons of the Casa del Rey Hotel. Car No. 20, placarded CASA DEL REY, was assigned to a special shuttle service operating exclusively between the hotel and the railroad depot. This run lasted for several years.

Although continuing as titular head of Coast Counties and Union Traction, Martin gradually retired from their active management, turning over the reins to Coleman. The younger man, well respected by the community, assumed the presidency of both companies in 1912. Robert L. Cardiff, Union's electrical engineer, succeeded him as manager of the traction company. Martin retired from Pacific Gas and Electric in 1914, returning to the Midwest a very wealthy man. At the time of his death—May 23, 1928—he headed the Mid-Continent Utilities Corporation, a company with extensive holdings in the Central and Southern states.

IT'S JULY 1911, and Fred Swanton's Casa del Rey Hotel has just opened its doors. Car No. 16 is westbound on Beach Street just past Cliff Street. Note that cars ran from the beach to Laveaga Park until the 1912 reorganization, after which Laveaga cars halted at Water and Pacific.
Randolph Brandt Collection

WITH OPENING of Casa del Rey, car No. 20 (left) was assigned permanent duty shuttling between the hotel and Union Station.
Vernon J. Sappers Historical Collection

TRUNDLING OVER the Water Street bridge, work motor No. 100 tows a carload of track laborers and material, probably during the building of the Laveaga Park branch.
Randolph Brandt Collection

Carbarn Interlude

(ABOVE) Union Traction's carbarn, at Pacific Avenue and Sycamore Street. (BELOW) Another view of the facility in about 1906, when tracks were still narrow-gauge. Seen in the barn are No. 4 and a wooden tower car.   *Both: Randolph Brandt Collection*

POWERHOUSE interior of the Union Traction carbarn shows a bank of motor-generator sets. At work in the carpenter shop, at the carbarn (below) are Clarence Fields (left), Ernest Fitzgerald (center), and Hugh Beauchamp. Young Fitzgerald was the son of George L. Fitzgerald, the company's master mechanic.   *Both: William Wulf Collection*

UNION TRACTION'S machine shop was a real "flapping belt" works, circa 1908. Carmen gathered at the barn for an informal portrait (below). Hats bore a "U.T. Co." legend and a company shield was worn on the lapel. *Both: William Wulf Collection*

THE POPULACE STILL FLOCKED to the electric cars in 1912, when No. 12 was snapped on Soquel at Pacific, looking east. At least one gentleman was saving his nickels by peddling a bicycle around town.

Randolph Brandt Collection

15. The Middle Years

BY 1912 Union Traction was carrying about a million passengers a year and maintaining service on three divisions: Capitola, Ocean Cliffs, and Laveaga Park. Capitola and Seabright cars of the Capitola Division terminated at Soquel and Pacific Avenues, where passengers transferred to the Vue de l'eau and beach cars of the Ocean Cliffs Division. The beachfront terminus was the Tent City Restaurant on the northeast corner of Beach and Cliff Streets, beneath the arches that spanned Beach Street connecting the Casa del Rey with the casino building. Cars to Laveaga Park departed every 20 minutes from Pacific Avenue and Water Street, the terminus of that division. Summertime schedules involved up to 18 cars. In the winter this number was usually cut back to six: three cars on the Ocean Cliffs Division, two on the Capitola Division, and one to Laveaga Park.

Richard M. Hotaling was now vice-president of the

company, with L.W. Pryor secretary and treasurer. J.C. Warren was engineer of the power station. George Fitzgerald was still the master mechanic, with J.H. Gill foreman. The company listed 19 motor cars and two trailers, operating over 14.34 miles of track. Its bonded indebtedness stood at $639,000, reflecting the additional monies poured into standard-gauging and expanding the system.

In 1913 the company asked permission to abandon its rails in Front Street and on the Riverside Avenue branch, offering to relinquish franchise rights to these routes. The Common Council on August 5 unanimously accepted quit-claim deeds; the rails were removed. The following year the city replaced its vintage-1882 Water Street (upper) bridge with a modern three-hinge, double-arch structure architecturally matched to the adjoining streetcar bridge. This entailed the company's moving its single-track line to the new span, as approved by ordinance September 15, 1914.

Financial affairs of Union Traction were now a matter of pressing concern to Coleman, who had since relocated from Santa Cruz to San Mateo. Ridership was up to about 1.3 million passengers annually, but the city's population, which more than doubled from 1900 to 1906, was holding at around 15,000. Furthermore, no dramatic increases were foreseen. Yearly interest on the indebtedness—$32,000—took about half the company's annual gross receipts, and payments were maintained only because Coleman refused to follow the customary guidelines for depreciating railroad properties (this plunged him into a running feud with officials of the State Railroad Commission). No further borrowing was possible.

Operations continued in this precarious fashion for the next three years, gross receipts remaining steady. Some economies were realized by cutting back schedules and reducing roadbed maintenance. Ridership dropped from 1.26 million in 1916 to 1.19 million in 1917. Then in 1918 it fell to 1.04 million; gross receipts dropped to a disastrous $57,000. Coleman gave up his argument with the railroad commission, and Union Traction stopped paying interest on its funded debt.

In May 1918 the company reported six cars in winter service, maintaining 15-minute headway on the Ocean Cliffs Division, 30-minute service to Twin Lakes and 60-minute service to Capitola on the Capitola Division, and 30-minute headway to Laveaga Park. Officials asked permission that month to raise fares from 5¢ to 6¢, the first such request by Union Traction. Approval was given in August. Some of the cars were rebuilt for one-man operation; others were scrapped. Operating personnel were reduced from 30 to 19. Ridership improved nearly 10% in 1919 and gross revenues climbed to more than $71,000, but the operation remained profitless. There was no money to improve equipment or roadbeds.

THIS WOODEN TRESTLE carried electric cars across the San Lorenzo River. No. 16 uses the Soquel Avenue span. *UCSC, Preston Sawyer Collection*

Despite all, Union Traction continued to have its fans. Josephine Clifford McCracklin, known locally as "the saviour of the big trees, the redeemer of the Big Basin, the progenitor of Sempervirons Park," reported her delight over a trip on the cars to Capitola in an article in the *Santa Cruz Surf* in 1918: "This is the age of joy rides. President and Mrs. (Woodrow) Wilson set the

WHEN IT RAINED, whoosh went the earth. A washout in 1912, at the curve from Twin Lakes trestle into 12th Avenue, halted service to Capitola (left), but crews soon were driving piles for a replacement bridge (right). *Both: Randolph Brandt Collection*

Figure 6

Santa Cruz Street Railways 1915

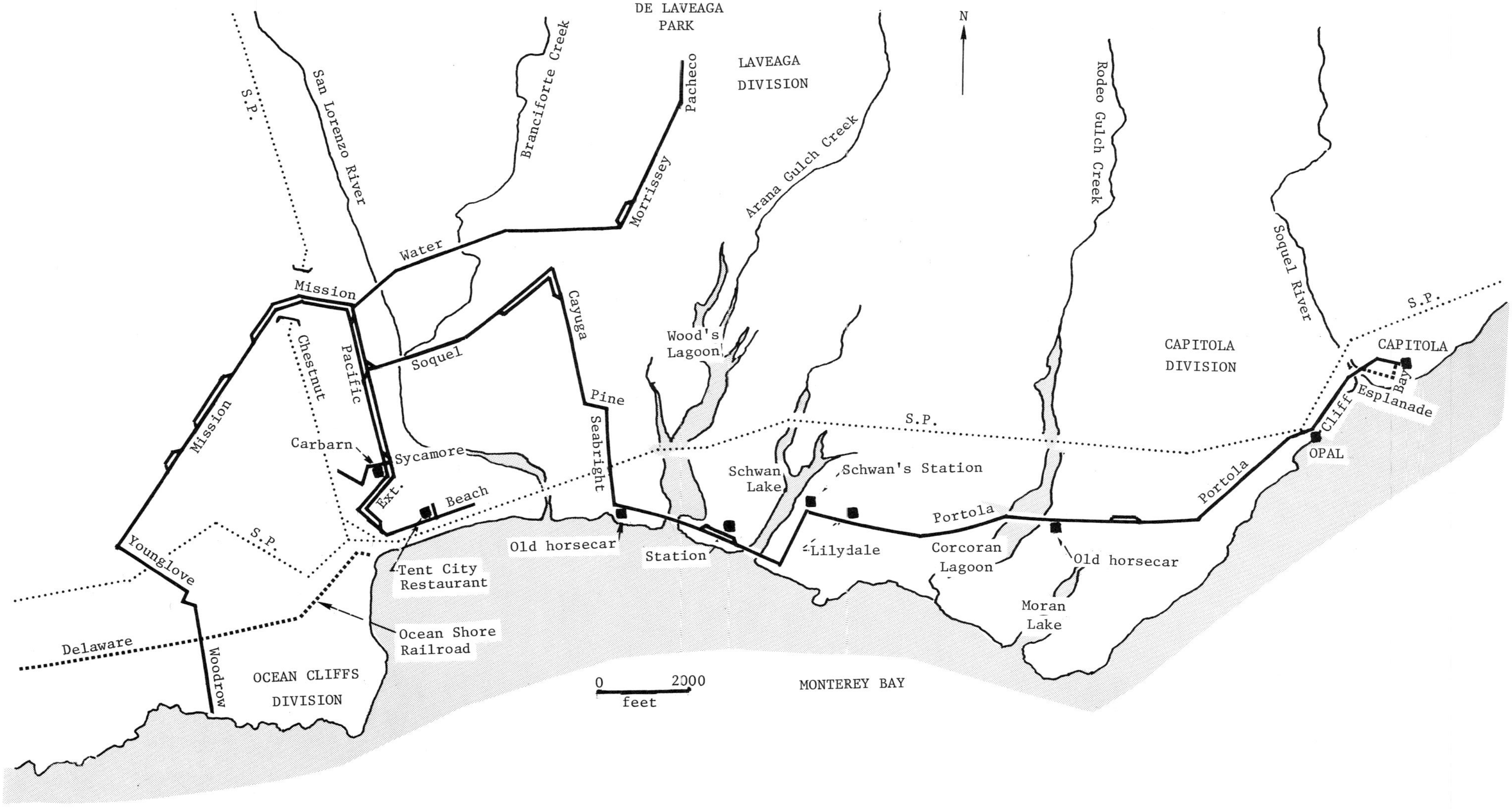

CONDUCTOR McNAMERA and tiny passenger on the Laveaga Park branch in the early 1920s.
Courtesy Nancy Lucking Sedon

highest example; (Navy) Secretary and Mrs. (Josephus) Daniels follow suit, and the whole Pacific Fleet with hundreds of admirals and hundred thousands of jolly tars are joy riding up and down our coast.

"That the joy ride craze extends to Europe is proved by the fact that the King and Queen of Belgium are about to take a trip to the United States; and it needs no special mention that the wealthy and well situated of these United States seem to have become chronic joy riders, preferably in their own touring cars. Santa Cruz is not behind in the number or quality of joy riders; in special Pullmans and private touring cars, my wealthy fellow citizens can joy ride with the best of them.

"But there are people in Santa Cruz who have no means to pay for a special Pullman or to buy a touring car and unfortunately I belong to this class. Not that I grieve over this; my tastes are naturally simple and I am quite happy when riding in a Union Traction streetcar. I can afford to pay streetcar fare and I believe in making the world more democratic.

"I have a joy ride to recommend for all classes, a really delightful ride which costs me exactly 24 cents, which is four cents more than it cost me before the war. . . .

". . . Here comes the Union Traction streetcar close up to the entrance of the Laveaga Park, and we are soon on our way down Morrissey Avenue and on Water

Street. It halts one moment at the corner of beautiful North Branciforte Avenue, where stands the handsome, solid Branciforte School, one of the many fine educational buildings in Santa Cruz. And as the car moves on, we glimpse for one moment the tall steeple of Holy Cross Church, built on the spot once occupied by the adobe church of Mission days.

"When we reach the Lower Plaza with its classic post-office building, we are given transfers for our six-cent tickets, and we rush along Pacific Avenue to Soquel Avenue, where we are given a transfer for our same six-cent carfare.

"Across the covered bridge we ride, much abused and railed at for its lack of beauty. Beauty is but skin deep, and in this case its lack is atoned for by the lovely far sights one enjoys while crossing it. A long, delightful, really enjoyable ride carries us through garden streets clear on to Seabright, where the song of the sea falls on the ear as the car speeds on to Twin Lakes. And here we pay six cents again, and do not regret the cost as the country rolls on toward Capitola.

"Country seats, farmhouses, dairies, ranches, summer resorts border the tracks of the Union Traction car, and the waters of the bay lie still and blue before us, as we near our destination, sometimes in the shadow of long, leafy avenues and borne across the placid surface of the river that flows into the sea at Capitola."

Randolph (Rudy) Brandt, longtime railfan and former employee of San Francisco's Market Street and Munici-

CARL LOUIS LUCKING posed most proudly in his motorman's uniform in 1918. *Courtesy Nancy Lucking Sedon*

pal railways, recalls those days fondly. Then a school-boy living at Twin Lakes, he depended on the cars to take him to and from Branciforte School. "Got off at Doyle Street and walked to school," he remembers. "Rode the Capitola cars, which had squeaky, high-pitched, shrill whistles like the Market Street Railway's work cars." Returning home he sometimes missed the Capitola car and took the Seabright local, walking down the tracks and over the bridge to reach Twin Lakes.

"We kids really took to the cars," he recalls. "We got to know the motormen and they knew us." One of his happiest recollections was getting to operate a car for a short distance, one quiet day, out near Lilydale. "The motorman let me swing the controller back and forth. I really felt like I was in charge."

Fares were not expensive for youngsters, who used school tokens. Yet some kids liked to nip rides on the cars. One motorman—a "rotund German," Brandt remembers—tried to get even with one gang by passing their stop. "The kids pulled the pole off the wire. Last thing I saw was the motorman chasing the kids down the right of way, swearing at them in German."

The streetcars also were fair game for youthful pranks. "Cars had to struggle coming up the grade from Capitola," he recalls, "and they had some trouble navigating the hill up from Wood's Lagoon. One Halloween, kids soaped the rails on Atlantic Avenue. Car made the grade and slipped around the corner, its wheels sparking all the way. Only thing that happened was that its pole came off the wire."

One gang moved a street-work barricade onto the Vue de l'eau track near Delaware Street. The next motorman out that branch assumed that track work was in progress, so he reversed direction and went back up Mission Street without going to the end of the line. The same thing happened to the next car. Finally the patrons waiting at Vue de l'eau called the company of-

REPAIRING A BROKEN wire span was a normal job for Union Traction's line crew, seen here along the Santa Cruz beachfront. Tower car 100 is followed by passenger trolley No. 12.   *Randolph Brandt Collection*

fice to ask why no cars were coming. Manager Cardiff removed the barricade and dispatched a special car to get them.

In April 1920 the company asked permission to further increase its one-way fares from 6¢ to 10¢, with tokens eight for 50¢ (close to the old rate). Soon thereafter, plans were announced to buy four one-man Birney "safety cars" to replace obsolete equipment. In November the company asked to cut the token rate

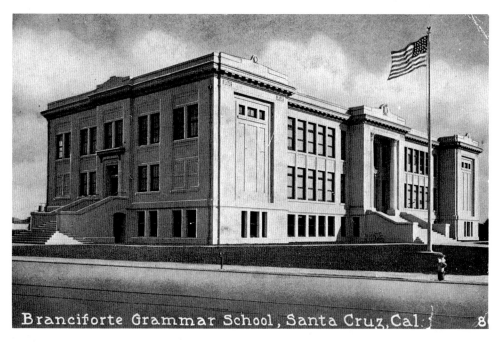

MANY STUDENTS of the Branciforte Grammar School arrived by trolley car. Tracks are seen in foreground in this 1918 view, though the retouchers have brushed away poles and wire.   *Randolph Brandt Collection*

Birney Safety Cars

BIRNEY CAR No. 24 (right) lays over on the Laveaga Park branch. Below, motorman poses aside No. 23.

Both: Harold Van Gorder Collection

FOUR BIRNEY Safety Cars, Nos. 21-24, arrived in 1922. No. 22 runs west along Beach Street on the beach-front, below.   *Randolph Brandt Collection*

AUTOMOTIVE AGE has arrived, and Birney No. 22 now competes with roadsters as the end of the system approaches.   *Vernon J. Sappers Historical Collection*

PACIFIC AVENUE at Soquel Street in 1920. Track turning right went to Twin Lakes-Capitola branch. *Randolph Brandt Collection*

TROLLEY TRACKS were prominent in this view of a parade up Mission Hill, 1917, which symbolized Santa Cruz's commitment to winning World War I.

Randolph Brandt Collection

THE CASINO on the beachfront is seen from the pier (ABOVE) in the early 1920s. A "Sacramento" car (BELOW) passes under the Casino archway en route from Casa del Rey Hotel. All these cars were retired before the last two years of streetcar operation.

Both: Randolph Brandt Collection

from eight to six for 50¢, with a double fare to Capitola. Both requests were granted in January 1921 as the result of an in-depth survey of the company's operations and prospects for successfully using the Birney cars. Reported the inspecting engineer to the State Railroad Commission: "From a study of conditions on the ground and a discussion with the management, I am convinced that there is no possibility of further important operating economies. The Gas and Electric Company makes a moderate charge for supervision and accounting and its forces attend to all the overhead electrical repairs. It also takes care of substation costs, delivering DC current.

"The tracks are not good enough to operate the four-wheel one-man cars, for I believe these cars would pitch and roll too much to take advantage of their higher speed. At present the cars are operated by one man (except for one swing man who acts as motorman through the business district on one line), so that there would result no economy in wages and I do not believe the principal remaining one-man economies resulting from less current consumption, from lower maintenance cost of cars, and from less track maintenance would warrant the purchase of one-man cars."

The engineer said he considered Union Traction's cars "well maintained and kept well painted. On the main line," he reported, "15-minute service is given, on the Laveaga Park line, 30 minutes, and on the Capitola line, hourly service. On the latter two lines but one car is used (on each), so it is obvious that reduction in service would result in discontinuance of operation on the line. Mr. Coleman stated that all three lines 'paid their way', so that there would be no advantage in discontinuance of any line or lines."

These opinions notwithstanding, the company bought four new cars in April 1922 at a cost of more than $25,000. These were single-truck, Birney safety cars, a type then popular all over the nation. The new cars proved popular and soon were a familiar sight along Pacific Avenue and down by the beach.

THIS SERIES OF PHOTOGRAPHS reconstructs Santa Cruz's most spectacular streetcar accident, August 21, 1921.

(RIGHT) Car No. 18, Capitola-bound, collided with an automobile at the east end of Soquel Avenue trestle. The motorman set the car in reverse and, with several passengers, alighted to render aid. Only Mrs. Hildreth Foster and her young son remained on board. Suddenly No. 18 started back across the trestle toward Pacific Avenue.

Randolph Brandt Collection

(BELOW) No. 18 gathered speed coming off the trestle and jumped the track at Soquel and Pacific, crashing into a parked coupe and toppling onto its side in front of the Orchid Sweet Shop. Mrs. Foster and son were thrown from the car, the woman suffering a skull fracture. The boy was not badly hurt.

UCSC, Preston Sawyer Collection

(LEFT, PAGE 92) Crowds gathered around overturned streetcar, blocking traffic. Car No. 30, beach-bound, stands waiting clearance to proceed.
UCSC, Preston Sawyer Collection

(ABOVE) Trucks—typical archbar equipment removed from old freight cars by Southern Pacific in Sacramento—remained upright in the street. Car No. 18 was reassembled and continued in service until 1926.
Randolph Brandt Collection

A summer mishap in 1921 proved to be Union Traction's most spectacular accident. Just before 11 o'clock Thursday morning, August 25, Car No. 18 left its terminus at the Trust Building corner, Soquel and Pacific Avenues, bound for Capitola. It crossed the trestle over the San Lorenzo, where the present concrete span was then being built to replace the covered bridge. At the Garfield-Riverside intersection, east end of the bridge, No. 18 collided with an automobile.

Motorman-conductor Claude Conlon stopped the car and jumped out, followed by several passengers who rendered aid to the three women motorists whose auto had overturned. Only Mrs. Hildreth Foster and her young son, of Blackburn Gulch, remained on the car.

Suddenly No. 18, which had been stopped abruptly with reverse applied, started rolling back toward town. Over the trestle it went, its trolley grinding sparks but refusing to jump the wire. The car gained momentum down the gentle incline toward Front Street. By the time it reached Pacific Avenue it was going at speed.

Rounding the corner sharply onto Pacific, it jumped the track and headed straight for the sidewalk in front of the Orchid Sweet Shop, crashing into a parked coupe. Swerving a little to the left, it shoved the coupe up against a telephone pole, toppling onto its side at the front door of the candy store. The unfortunate Mrs. Foster and her youngster were thrown from the back platform onto the sidewalk in front of the Walsh-Mellott shoe store. She suffered a skull fracture from which she later recovered. The boy was not badly hurt.

Strangely enough, the unmanned streetcar struck no one en route to the accident and grazed only one automobile, near Front Street. The car body was ripped from its trucks when it turned over. The trucks remained upright on the street.

Officer Mike Curry and others of the city police stayed at the scene for the rest of the day, keeping onlookers from jamming the busy intersection. Car No. 18 was reassembled and remained in service until 1926.

16. Final Days for Streetcars

COAST COUNTIES' fortunes were on the upturn in the early 1920s. In 1922 Coleman took over gas and electric plants in Gilroy. The following year he merged his Contra Costa Gas Company, formed in 1914, into Coast Counties.

Union Traction remained in perilous straits. Its rolling stock by midyear 1922 consisted of the Birneys plus two open cars, three closed cars, and five combinations all beginning to deteriorate. True to the inspection engineer's prediction, the roadbed's rundown condition hampered operation of the Birneys. Service became marginal. Coleman was also locked in a dispute with the State Railroad Commission about the company's valuation, claiming on a replacement basis that it was now worth $900,000 or more compared with about $560,000 in 1915. The Railroad Commission put the present worth at around $300,000. This determination had important bearing on the amount of depreciation Coleman could charge.

More damaging, however, was that Santa Cruz, like most other California communities, was experiencing an onrush of automobile traffic. Streets were congested, and ridership was fast declining. The Common Council pledged itself to a program of hard-surfacing the city streets and brought pressure on Union Traction to pave between its rails and two feet on each side as required by its franchises. Coleman branded the paving requirements impossible to meet, unsuccessfully sought relief from the city, and finally took his plea to the voters. Some 2,445 townspeople turned out February 28, 1923, for a special election at which—by a narrow 143-vote plurality—they passed a charter amendment lifting this responsibility. The company claimed no special public-relations effort except for widespread publicity of four facts: (1) that Union Traction had never paid a dividend; (2) that the company had not paid interest on its indebtedness for six years, its bonds now selling at 10¢ or less on the dollar; (3) that company officials were serving without pay, and (4) that the company stood ready any time to give itself to the city at no charge.

Despite passage of the charter amendment, which was later ratified by the State Legislature, the Common Council refused to grant the paving exemption. Coleman responded March 1924 by asking the State Railroad Commission for rights to abandon rail service on the Laveaga Park and Capitola branches, substituting bus service. In August the Commission approved both abandonments; in September the Common Council followed suit for Laveaga Park only. To the *Santa Cruz News* these proceedings made little sense: "Thus will the charter amendment, designed to encourage the Union Traction Company to keep its lines going, become of no practical avail. The question raised by this attitude of the administration will soon be settled, for when the

tracks are removed and the space leveled off it will be up to the property owners to pave the streets from curb to curb and pay all the expense."

Starting in November, the company scrapped one closed car and all five combinations, leaving just eight cars in service: the Birneys, two open cars (for summer service), one closed car, and the work and tower car. Two of three 25-passenger Mack buses on order were delivered December 8, the last day that streetcars ran to either Capitola or Laveaga Park. On December 9 the new buses began operating on an hourly schedule to

Capitola via Water, Morrissey, and Pacheco, serving the patrons of both branches. "Capitola is most enthusiastic about the fine new bus line," reported the *News* three days later. "Many people are trying them just for the interesting trip."

Bus service supplanted streetcars December 12 on the Soquel Avenue-Twin Lakes line. The last car was taken off at 3:51 P.M. and sent to the shops; a new bus stood by, waiting to make the next regular trip. A half-hour headway was established. Manager Cardiff announced that the buses would run on regular schedules

THE MAYOR APPEARED to pose with the "old" and the "new." Santa Cruz Mayor John Maher stands in front of Birney Safety Car No. 23 which completed the last Laveaga Park run on December 8, 1924. Union Traction's bus No. 1, just arrived from the Mack factory that day, is at left. *Randolph Brandt Collection*

"just the same as streetcars and give just as good service, with the advantage of alighting passengers at the curb instead of in the middle of the street." Just eight days later, also, the company experienced its first bus accident, as related by the *News:* "One of the new Mack buses, recently put on the Seabright and Twin Lakes run, was badly damaged Saturday when it collided with a grader near Schwan station. A great dent and other scratches and slight tears to the body were caused by the collision. This morning (December 22) it was announced from the Union Traction Company barns that no interruption in their East Side passenger schedule was necessitated by the collision. The injured bus is again running today, with all necessary repair work being done at night in the barns."

Workmen began removing the rails from Soquel Avenue and elsewhere on the Laveaga Park and Capitola branches. Even as this work was proceeding, the State Railroad Commission was considering another request from Coleman, filed the previous October, to halt service on the Ocean Cliffs line beyond the Lower Plaza. Permission was granted in February 1925, but city officials blocked this abandonment, telling the company in effect either to keep all remaining lines in operation (and pave the streets) or abandon rail service altogether. Coleman chose the latter, filing in April to end streetcar service from the Lower Plaza to the casino.

Negotiations continued all summer. Accord was finally reached, the city agreeing to the abandonment of streetcars and the company agreeing to remove track, trolley, and appurtenances, pave the vacated streets, and post a $25,000 bond through Coast Counties to guarantee its performance. The company also consented to maintain bus service. These terms were stipulated in city ordinances of August and November 1925. The Railroad Commission agreed in August to streetcar abandonment on Pacific Avenue.

"Take your last look at the streetcars on Pacific Avenue today," advised the *Sentinel* on January 14, 1926. "Tomorrow they will be no more. At midnight workmen will start the removal of the trolley over the avenue, and as the sun sends forth its rays at dawn (in Santa Cruz, where tule frogs hold sway), Old Sol will look down upon a city that takes the lead in modern motor transportation. Automobile buses will tomorrow replace the streetcars. People residing on side streets no doubt saw the buses being driven about yesterday and the drivers were the motormen of streetcar days. It is different guiding a car along a track than steering an automobile.

"Later the tracks will be removed from Pacific Avenue and other thoroughfares improved. Santa Cruz is one of the few cities in the United States to have a complete system of motor transportation."

All went according to schedule. At midnight the last streetcar, a Birney, left the beach with Lee Baldwin as motorman-conductor, arriving a few minutes later at the Sycamore Street carbarn. It was the last car to move in the city, ending more than 50 years of streetcar service. Hours later, on the morning of January 15, motor buses took over.

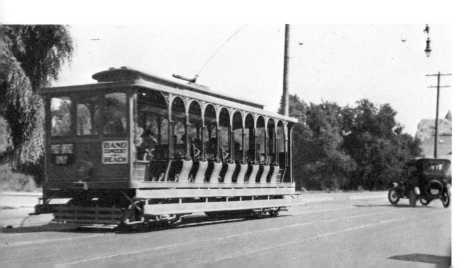

TWO OPEN BENCH TROLLEYS survived until the final closure of streetcar operation. Car No. 30 (above) is northbound on Pacific near Soquel Avenue. Seen at left along Pacific Avenue, between Cathcart and Laurel, is open car No. 31. *Both: Vernon J. Sappers Historical Collection*

THE NEW ERA in Santa Cruz transit came on wheels of rubber. These three Mack buses, each seating 25 passengers, were Union Traction's initial fleet of rubber-tired passenger vehicles, arriving in December 1924 to take over the Laveaga, Twin Lakes and Capitola branches. (Black outline at top is missing portion of negative.) *Randolph Brandt Collection*

17. Epilogue

RAILS, WIRES, and appurtenances were removed and pavement laid in the city streets, hiding most traces of the streetcars. The Birneys were sold to Bakersfield and the other cars scrapped. But all was not over. In September 1926 Union Traction applied to the State Railroad Commission for permission to abandon the Capitola and Twin Lakes motor coach lines, drawing angry blasts from city officials. Instead, the company sold its motor coaches and franchise routes to the Auto Transit Company, which got approval from the Common Council in January 1927 to operate the bus service.

Coast Counties retained the old carbarn at Pacific Avenue and Sycamore Street and, in 1927, wrote off nearly $1 million in investment as a result of its rail abandonments. S. Waldo Coleman sold the utility company in 1928 to the Pacific Public Service Company, which later became a subsidiary of the Standard Oil Company of California until merged into Pacific Gas and Electric. Coleman also retired in 1928 as president of the Santa Cruz Seashore Company, although continued as principal stockholder until the company was sold in 1946 to a group of Santa Cruzans. He died in March 1972 at Stanford Hospital, in his ninetieth year.

Auto Transit operated briefly in Santa Cruz, then gave way to the Pickwick Stages System, an SP subsidiary. According to Nancy Sedon, daughter of Carl Lucking, all drivers were required to buy and wear regulation gray uniforms and to buy expensive Southern Pacific-approved railway watches. Lucking drove for both Union Traction and Pickwick.

In June 1930, Pickwick sold out its Santa Cruz operations to Ralph L. Heple, a former Pickwick driver, who operated the service under his own name. Heple died in 1934, his widow Ora B. Heple continuing to operate the company, with John Foster as manager. (Foster was active in its management until his death in 1962.) By the 1940s the name of the operation was changed to *Santa Cruz Transit Company*. Mrs. Heple remarried in 1946 and with her new husband, Chester R. Smith, continued with operations, struggling with mounting costs and declining revenues that hit most city bus systems following the end of World War II.

Santa Cruz Transit curtailed its schedules in March 1962, the Smiths citing a 15% drop in revenue the previous month as compared with February 1961 ($4,347 vs. $4,809). This was followed in August 1964 by further cuts and then an offer by the Smiths to give the

Empty Right-of-Way

AT VUE DE L'EAU, in 1927. Only the center median strip (above) is a reminder that streetcars once served Woodrow Avenue. Union Traction bus at right. *Randolph Brandt Collection*

UNION TRACTION BUS sits at end of Wood's Lagoon bridge, closed for reconstruction.
Randolph Brandt Collection

company to any responsible operator. Losses, they claimed, now amounted to $1,000 a month. Santa Cruz city and county, and the City of Capitola jointly agreed to underwrite these losses. Service was thus maintained while local officials drafted plans for a countywide transit district with taxing authority. Voters gave their blessing in November 1968; the *Santa Cruz Metropolitan Transit District* was formed February 20, 1969, and took over operations in 1970.

Since then, from a modest $30,000 budget and service obtained from the Smiths at 57½¢ a mile, the SCMTD has grown to an extensive system with 27 different bus routes. (Santa Cruz Transit Company contin-

ues as a charter bus operator, still owned by Mr. and Mrs. Smith.) SCMTD ridership has increased 700% since 1970, to an annual total of 2.219 million (1975-76). Fares remain low: 25¢ for a single ride, commuter books available. Annual operating expenses of $1.54 million are met by fares, county tax revenues, direct taxation (5¢ per $100 assessed valuation), and Federal matching funds under the Urban Mass Transportation Act of 1964. Riders now find it possible to travel on one fare from Boulder Creek and Scott's Valley in the north to Watsonville in the far southeast. This is a comprehensive transit system beyond the dreams of even the staunchest traction supporters in their heyday.

ALAS, THEIR DAY IS PAST! The body of car No. 20 (left, above) became a garden outbuilding, while No. 17's frame (right, above) rotted away on a 7th Avenue farm north of the Southern Pacific track.   *Both: Randolph Brandt Collection*

IN HIGH BOOTS and Sam Brown belt, Carl Lucking poses in his bus driver's uniform (also see photograph on page 87). Mr. Lucking obtained a California operator's license for his new role on the buses. In these simpler times the license (reproduced full size) was mailed to the holder like a postcard (bottom, left).   *All: Courtesy Nancy Lucking Sedon*

STATE OF CALIFORNIA
DIVISION OF MOTOR VEHICLES
OPERATOR'S LICENSE   No. ★ S10007

THIS CERTIFIES *that the undersigned operator has this* 3
day of AUG 19 23 *been licensed to operate motor vehicles in accordance with the provisions of Chapter 147, Statutes 1919.*

DESCRIPTION

Age 43	Sex MALE
Height 5' 6"	Weight 180
Color Eyes HAZEL	Color Hair AUBURN

DIVISION OF MOTOR VEHICLES   By HB

Carl L. Lucking

This card is good until revoked, when signed by the operator to whom it is issued   *Signature of Operator*

CARL L LUCKING
55 ROONEY ST
SANTA CRUZ CALIF

Motor Bus

HEPLE TRANSPORTATION CO. No. 4 posed when new in the 1940s (left). It was a Ford Transit bus (built by the same Ford Motor Co. which populated the nation's streets with its Model Ts, Model As, and V-8s).
Motor Bus Society

SANTA CRUZ Transit Company bus No. 2 (right) ran along Beach Street in 1948. The automobile following is a De Soto, a now-extinct Chrysler product.
Robert A. Burrowes

SCTCo bus No. 3 (below), an early-model Ford bus wth front engine, runs amongst the vacant lots of the Live Oak District, in 1948.
Robert A. Burrowes

Driver Gardner poses in front of bus No. 6 (left) at County Hospital, circa 1948.
Robert A. Burrowes

Decades

A LATER GENERATION of Santa Cruz Transit Company bus was General Motors-built No. 16, seen crossing the Southern Pacific tracks at 17th Avenue in 1961, right.
Robert A. Burrowes

CARRYING PATRONS along Seabright Avenue, at Windham, bus No. 10 is viewed, also in 1961 (below). *Robert A. Burrowes*

TRANSIT WAS ALIVE IN Santa Cruz in 1977; here are two views of the Santa Cruz Metropolitan Transit District. Bus No. 830 loads passengers at the downtown Transit Center, on Soquel Avenue near Pacific Avenue (above, right). Along Soquel Avenue, bus No. 826 heads downtown (below). The Capitola electric cars turned right onto Cayuga St. on their way to Twin Lakes and Capitola in the later years of streetcar service.
Both: Jim Walker

A GALLERY of 1977 Santa Cruz views, all taken by author Charles S. McCaleb. (Left) Lower Plaza (Front Street at left, Pacific Avenue at right). The Teacup Restaurant is in Hugo Hihn's 1860 Flatiron building. Pacific Avenue has now been converted into a garden mall with specialty shops and restaurants. (Right) Santa Cruz Union Station, now converted to an eating establishment. Hopper cars are in SP yards.

(LEFT) Bay Street overpass over S.P. track at original cut for the Santa Cruz Railroad. Looking roughly northwesterly. Tracks branch; left to Davenport, right into yards and station. (RIGHT) Pacific Avenue looking northward from Beach Hill. Prolo Chevrolet is at former carbarn site (Sycamore and Pacific).

(LEFT) From the foot of Atlantic Avenue looking east across the mouth of Wood's Lagoon. Wagon bridge and Union Traction bridge spanned the mouth of what is now the Yacht Harbor. (RIGHT) View across mouth of Yacht Harbor (same location as photo on left) toward East Cliff Drive.

(RIGHT) The view from Opal Cliffs toward Capitola. Union Traction's line ran down the bluff (Portola Drive, today) at the left.

(BELOW) Downtown Capitola; white building in center is on site of the streetcar station (compare with view on page 76).
Both: Charles S. McCaleb

(RIGHT) Casa del Rey still functions in 1977, as a retirement residence.

(BELOW) The Santa Cruz Transit Company garage on Pacific Avenue now houses the company's charter buses.
Both: Jim Walker

(BELOW, RIGHT) The remains of old Twin Lakes trestle are still visible at low tide. This photograph was taken in 1975 by *Harold Van Gorder.*

EAST SANTA CRUZ HORSECAR shows the name of builder Evan Lukens on its side, beneath the floorboard. Lukens was a local blacksmith and wheelwright whose shop was on Park Street (later Union Street) just east of what is now Center Street.

Harold Van Gorder Collection

Rolling Stock
Descriptions and Car Rosters

Tracing the origins and service lives of the streetcars of Santa Cruz is very frustrating. Larger operations in other cities kept better records that survived because those companies were still active in recent years and ran the cars pretty much "as is" during their service lives.

This was not true in Santa Cruz, where both the cars and company disappeared rather early, the equipment passed through many corporate changes in which numbers may have been changed, propulsion went from horses to electrics, the track gauge changed, and no one apparently kept track of all this.

Horsecars

City Railroad Company

Commenced operation August 1875 with two wooden-bodied horsecars that may have been of local manufacture, perhaps by Thomas and Martin Carter who were then building bridges and work cars for the Santa Cruz Railroad. Wheels and cast parts possibly were produced by the Amner Foundry on River Street, Santa Cruz. The horsecars were painted and lettered locally. No roster nor record of the final disposition of these cars has been found.

Pacific Avenue Street Railroad Company

Commenced operation in 1877 with horsecars not of local origin (probably obtained from San Francisco). Additional cars were added in 1879 and 1880 (one built in the latter year was an "open palace

car" from San Francisco that cost $606). In 1883 three cars were obtained from local builder Evan Lukens. All equipment was repaired, repainted, and fitted with new wheels and running gear in 1888. Wheels and cast parts were undoubtedly from the Amner Foundry. In 1891 the company listed nine cars, of which four (Nos. 2, 3, 5 and 7) have been identified from photographs. Plans were discussed for using two or more of these cars as trailers for the *Santa Cruz, Garfield Park, and Capitola Electric Railway;* this may have occurred briefly, but more likely the cars were sold to the *East Santa Cruz Street Railroad Company.*

East Santa Cruz Street Railroad Company

Commenced operation May 1890 with three horsecars by local builder Evan Lukens: two open (Nos. 1 and 2) and one closed (No. 3). In 1892 the company listed 14 cars—the fleet had shrunk to eight cars by 1901. Trucks from some of these cars were used on work cars of the *Santa Cruz, Capitola and Watsonville Electric Railway* in 1903 during construction of its line to Capitola. Several ESCStRR horsecar bodies became way stations for the Santa Cruz, Capitola and Watsonville line. One served as a waiting room at the Garfield Park tabernacle, according to William Wulf.

Three cars (Nos. 1, 2 and 4) have been identified from photographs.

The *East Santa Cruz Street Railroad Company* also briefly operated a steam dummy (locomotive), the "Wm. Ely," built by the Baldwin Locomotive Works, Philadelphia, in 1895. No photos are known to exist nor any record of its final disposition (its track gauge of 3 feet, 2¼ inches probably made it hard to sell).

THE SHADOW OF conductor Albert S. McCormick, at left, is reflected in the shiny wood siding of Capitola electric car No. 9, at Capitola.
Courtesy Alberta McCormick and Margaret Koch

Narrow-Gauge Electric Cars

Santa Cruz, Garfield Park, and Capitola Electric Railway

Commenced operation November 1891 with two closed motor cars and two open trailers, with hand and foot brakes, equipped with Thomson-Houston (a General Electric predecessor) electrical components. It seems probable that the cars were built at the Holt Bros. Stockton Combine Harvester & Agricultural Works in Stockton, Calif. All had single trucks. In March 1892 the company added new open cars with an aisle down the center. These evidently had double trucks. Three cars (Nos. 1, 6, and 7) have been identified from photographs. All equipment became the property of the *Santa Cruz Electric Railway* in August 1892 as the result of a merger.

Santa Cruz Electric Railway

Commenced operation August 1892 with the rolling stock of the *Santa Cruz, Garfield Park, and Capitola Electric Railway.* The closed motor cars were double-trucked in December 1892, and the open trailers were motorized in March 1893. Eight cars, all motorized, were listed as the company's roster in 1896; two more cars, added early in 1904 (origin not known), completed this company's fleet. Three cars (Nos. 5, 6, and 7) have been identified from photographs. All equipment became the property of the *Union Traction Company* in October 1904 as the result of a merger. Probable roster:

Nos.	Builder & Date	Comments
1-2	Stockton, 1891	Closed motors, double-trucked in 1892
3-4	Stockton, 1891	Open trailers, motorized in 1893
5-8	Unknown, 1892	Open motor cars
9-10	St. Louis Car Co.	Probably open motor, date unknown

(ABOVE) Capitola electric car No. 12 at Vue de l'eau after amalgamation. *UCSC, Preston Sawyer Collection*

(BELOW, LEFT) Private car of the Capitola line is thought to be the first trolley to enter Capitola, October 4, 1904. *Randolph Brandt Collection*

Santa Cruz, Capitola and Watsonville Railway Company

Commenced operation June 1903 with equipment apparently ordered the same time as *Monterey and Pacific Grove Electric Railway* cars Nos. 1-4 (St. Louis Car Company orders 344-346 dated November 11, 1902, called for two 10-bench open cars, two double-truck closed cars and one double-truck private car). In that month the company listed **eight** cars (two open bench, five combinations, and one parlor car) and the source of the units not covered in the St. Louis Car records is not known. Additional cars were added (again, source not known) in August 1903. All motor cars were equipped with two 40-horsepower Westinghouse motors; Taylor and Bemis trucks were used. Of the total, two were indicated as trailers. Six cars (Nos. 8, 9, 11, 12, 14 and the parlor car) have been confirmed from photographs. All equipment became the property of the *Union Traction Company* in the 1904 merger. Tentative roster:

Nos.	Builder & Date	Comments
7 & 8	St. Louis, 1903	Open-bench motor cars
9	St. Louis, 1903	Open-bench motor car, single-truck
10-14	St. Louis, 1903	Combination (open-closed) motor cars
18	St. Louis, 1903	Combination (open-closed) motor car
Parlor	St. Louis, 1903	Closed, double-truck motor car

Union Traction Company

This was the "end product" of the merger of the *Santa Cruz Electric Railway* and the *Santa Cruz, Capitola and Watsonville Railway Company* and operated Santa Cruz' street railway system from October 1904 until its demise in January 1926. In January 1905 the company listed 18 motor cars and two trailers and new cars were added later that year. It seems probable that the original Stockton-built equipment from the *Santa Cruz Electric Railway* was retired during this time. In March 1907 Union Traction was still listing 18 St. Louis-built motor cars and two trailers. There was also one wooden work and tower car, apparently of local origin. These cars evidently were sold or otherwise disposed of during standard-gauging of the system in 1907, although some may have been fitted with standard-gauge trucks and used briefly during the transition. Lack of a specific roster makes it impossible to say for sure that any of the narrow-gauge cars survived as some of the cars shown on the standard-gauge roster.

Further notes:

Margaret Koch, of the *Santa Cruz Sentinel*, reports that car No. 8 was bought by Mrs. Elizabeth Thiel for $20 and used for many years as a streetcar cottage next to the Episcopal Church in Capitola.

The Westinghouse and Walker traction motors from these cars were retained in the company inventory for many years.

NARROW GAUGE Union Traction car No. 4 at Tent City Restaurant. The fate of most narrow-gauge cars after the tracks were widened is a mystery.
UCSC, Preston Sawyer Collection

FIVE STANDARD GAUGE cars built for Union Traction in the Sacramento Gas & Electric shops, featured a unique rope braking system. No. 5 is seen at Vue de l'eau.
Vernon J. Sappers Historical Collection

Standard-Gauge Electric Cars

Union Traction Company commenced standard-gauge operations September 1907, with five cars built in the 28th and M Street shops of the Sacramento Gas & Electric Company (these were among 28 cars built for California street railway systems by SG&E—later Pacific Gas & Electric—from 1902 to 1909). Including these, the company acquired 19 cars between May 1907 and July 1908 (many of which were probably former narrow-gauge cars modified by Union Traction). Most were converted to one-man operation immediately following World War I and most had been scrapped by December 1924. In April 1922 the company ordered four single-truck Birney Safety Cars that remained in service until closure of the system in 1926. There is some evidence that the company once had two trailers of unknown origin. Much of the following roster is based on official documents that unfortunately show little information on building dates to assist in tracing origins:

No.	Builder	Year	Comments	Motors	Scrapped
1	Sacramento Gas & Electric	1907	California (open-closed), double-truck	GE	February 1923
2	do.	do.	do. (Note 1 for cars 1 to 5)	do.	May 1919
3	do.	do.	do.	do.	February 1923
4	do.	do.	do.	Walker	March 1922
5	do.	do.	do.	GE	February 1923
11	St. Louis Car Co.	unk.	do.	do.	December 1924
12	do.	unk.	do.	do.	do.
14	do.	unk.	Closed, double-truck	do.	do.
15	do.	unk.	Closed, double-truck (Note 2)	do.	November 1924
16	Holt Bros.	unk.	California (open-closed) double-truck (Note 3)	do.	December 1924
17	Union Traction Co.	unk.	California, double-truck (see Note 4)	do.	November 1924
18	St. Louis Car Co.	unk.	Closed, double-truck	do.	1926
19	Carter Brothers	unk.	California, double-truck	Walker	March 1922
20	Hammond	1886	(Note 5)	GE	June 1921
21 (2nd)	do.	do.	(Note 5)	Walker	June 1921
21	American Car Co.	1922	Birney Safety Car, single-truck (Note 6)	GE	(Note 6)
22	do.	do.	do.	do.	do.
23	do.	do.	do.	do.	do.
24	do.	do.	do.	do.	do.
30	Unknown	unk.	Open-bench car, double-truck	do.	1926
31	do.	do.	do. (Nos. 30 & 31 had arch-bar trucks)	do.	do.
41	Holt Brothers	do.	do.	Walker	February 1922
100	Unknown	do.	Work/Tower car. Probably home-built.		1926

Notes on Union Traction Company roster:

1. Cars Nos. 1-5 were equipped with a unique, SG&E-developed rope brake, which consisted of a steel drum mounted on the unmotored axle in each truck, around which were mounted three coils of 1¼″ manila hemp rope. One end of this rope was attached to a large brake lever located at the motorman's position at each end of the car; the other was attached to the brake rigging. When the motorman pulled back on the brake lever, the rope, due to the forward momentum of the car, cinched tightly around the drum. The archbar trucks had been reworked for this use by SG&E from old Southern Pacific freight car trucks! There is some evidence that car No. 4 was equipped with Walker motors whereas the others had General Electric types.

2. Had split sash, meaning the windows could be opened.

3. Cars shown as built by Holt Brothers were constructed at that firm's Stockton Combine Harvester & Agricultural Works.

4. Probably rebuilt by the company from an old horsecar. Featured rope brakes as on cars Nos. 1-5 (see Note 1 above). Body ended up on a farm on Seventh Avenue north of the Southern Pacific tracks.

5. Cars 20 and 21 had a long history. They were originally built as Omnibus cable cars, then acquired by San Francisco's United Railways about 1886 and rebuilt in that company's 28th & Valencia carhouse about 1898 as single-truck California-type electric cars. The two cars were later sold to Union Traction Co. They were known locally as "dinkies." Specifications: weight 19,000 pounds, length 25′0″, width 8′0″, Brill No. 21 truck, 24″ wheels, two General Electric 52 motors, K2 control, 24 seats. The body of No. 20 ended up as an outbuilding in Santa Cruz.

6. Total cost of cars Nos. 21-24 was $25,252. All were sold to the Bakersfield & Kern electric railway in 1927, where they became Nos. 16-19. B&K Nos. 17 and 19 were resold to Nova Scotia Light & Power Co., Halifax, N.S., in 1942 after closure of the Bakersfield streetcar lines, where they continued to operate until 1949. Specifications: weight 16,600 pounds, length 28′0″, width 7′8″, Brill 79El truck, two 25-horsepower motors, 30 seats. Builder's order number 1302.

(LEFT) Car No. 2 sits on Beach Street between Main and the wharf, west of the casino. Note the Southern Pacific Railway Post Office car in the background.
UCSC, Preston Sawyer Collection

(BELOW, LEFT) Sacramento car No. 2 at the end of Woodrow Avenue (Vue de l'eau).
McFarland Photo; Randolph Brandt Collection

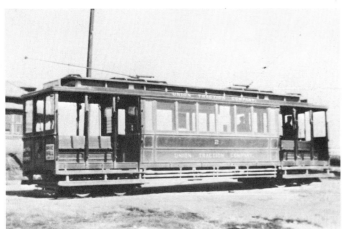

(ABOVE, RIGHT) In later years, the company shops closed up the open sections of the cars for one-man service; economical, but hardly flattering to the lines of the cars.
Randolph Brandt Collection

(LEFT) An end view of No. 3 shows construction details of the "Sacramento" cars. It is on the beach run; photo looks west from Main Street.
Vernon J. Sappers Historical Collection

108

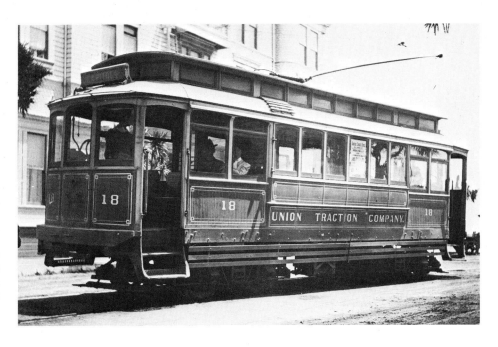

(RIGHT) St. Louis Car Company built all-closed car No. 18, which operated until the end of the system. The handsome car is seen beside Hotel Capitola, on the Capitola loop.
Vernon J. Sappers Historical Collection

(BELOW) At the terminus of the Laveaga Park branch, No. 19 awaits its next circuit in and out of town.
Vernon J. Sappers Historical Collection

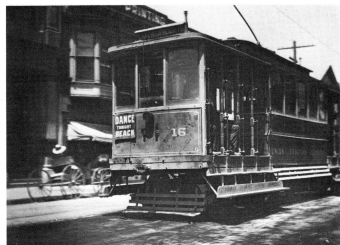

(ABOVE, RIGHT) A closeup view shows details of No. 16's fancy woodwork. Three slats along the side were supposed to prevent unwary pedestrians from falling into the wheels and slat wood basket under the end was designed to scoop up anybody falling down in front of approaching car.
Vernon J. Sappers Historical Collection

(RIGHT) Ornate open bench car No. 30 was a summer favorite. It could haul huge crowds.
Randolph Brandt Collection

THE TOWER CAR, No. 100, was on Mission Hill working on the overhead when the photographer asked the crew to pose. Crew chief is George L. Fitzgerald (in black suit and hat), former master mechanic and carbarn supervisor at this time. Fitzgerald's son Ernest also worked for Union Traction. The utility car was probably home-built.
Randolph Brandt Collection

MODIFIED FOR one-man service, No. 18's rear door was sealed. It is seen at Twin Lakes.
Vernon J. Sappers Historical Collection

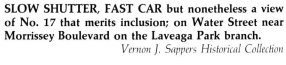

SLOW SHUTTER, FAST CAR but nonetheless a view of No. 17 that merits inclusion; on Water Street near Morrissey Boulevard on the Laveaga Park branch.
Vernon J. Sappers Historical Collection

AN EARLIER VIEW of No. 17, on Water Street, shows it before modifications that are shown on the photograph above and at right. This scene is circa 1917. The car was probably a company rebuild from a horsecar.
Randolph Brandt Collection

Brief Biographical Notes

The following information is derived mostly from contemporary newspaper accounts (biographies, death notices, etc.). Its completeness and accuracy cannot be assured. It is meant as a guide and supplement to county histories and other materials available through the public libraries in Santa Cruz, Santa Clara, and Monterey counties, including the following:

Coleman, Charles M., *P.G. and E. of California.* New York: McGraw-Hill, 1952.

Gudde, Erwin G., *California Place Names.* Berkeley: University of California Press, 1969.

Guinn, J.M., *History of the State of California and Biographical Record of Santa Cruz, San Benito, Monterey and San Luis Obispo Counties.* Chicago: The Chapman Publishing Co., 1903.

Harrison, E.S., *History of Santa Cruz County.* San Francisco: Pacific Press Co., 1892.

Harrison, E.S., *Santa Cruz County, 1890.* San Francisco: Pacific Press Co., 1890.

Koch, Margaret, *Santa Cruz County: Parade of the Past.* Fresno, California: Valley Publishers, 1973.

MacGregor, Bruce, *South Pacific Coast.* Berkeley: Howell-North Books, 1968.

Martin, Edward, *History of Santa Cruz County, California, with Biographical Sketches.* Los Angeles: Historic Record Co., 1911.

Anthony, Elihu. b. New York 1818; to Santa Clara 1847 and Santa Cruz 1848. Methodist minister; hardware merchant; first Santa Cruz postmaster; first chairman Santa Cruz County Board of Supervisors. Built first Santa Claus foundry (said to be the third foundry built in California). Reportedly first in California to make picks for miners. Helped organize town's first Protestant church. Helped build town's first wharf (1855). It is said that Anthony, for the sum of $3.62½ (the cost for filing a deed), acquired a good-sized piece of land on the "flat" stretching along the San Lorenzo River and later subdivided this property, selling lots for $100 each in what is now the city center.

Barnet, Zacha. b. San Francisco 1862; d. Santa Cruz April 21, 1904. Came to Santa Cruz as a child. Was city editor for the *Sentinel* for 20 years.

Blackburn, William. d. Santa Cruz March 26, 1867. Cabinetmaker, woodworker, first *alcalde* of Santa Cruz, state assemblyman from Santa Cruz 1855. Acquired property and reportedly became first Santa Cruz millionaire. Survived for several decades by his wife, Harriet Meade Blackburn, a Massachusetts woman.

Brazer, John. b. Massachusetts 1825; d. Santa Cruz January 11, 1907. To Santa Cruz in late 1860s; clerk 1867; opened first book and stationery store. Santa Cruz postmaster 1880. Director Bank of Santa Cruz County 1881. Director City Bank 1901. Graduate Dartmouth College; close personal friend Dr. S.H. Willey and his nephew Henry; bachelor; no known relatives at time of death.

Carter, John Stone. b. New Hampshire 1828. Grain dealer San Jose, Santa Clara County 1866.

Clark, Dr. Hulbert H. General manager Nevada County Electric Power Company, with Eugene de Sabla, September 1892. Mayor Santa Cruz 1896-98.

Cole, Thomas. b. New York 1828; d. San Francisco June 30, 1904. President Bullion Mining Company; president Chollar Mining Company.

Coleman, John C. b. England 1823; emigrated to U.S.; settled in California in late 1850s or early 1860s, living in Grass Valley. Was successful, with brother, in developing gold properties; relocated to San Francisco with a sizeable fortune. With Eugene de Sabla and Richard M. Hotaling, was board member 1900 of Bay Counties Power Company, which built 40,000-volt transmission line from Colgate Powerhouse on Yuba River via Woodland and Carquinez Strait to Oakland. With de Sabla, Hotaling, and John Martin, board member 1902 of Valley Counties Power Company. With same associates, an incorporator and later a board member (1903) of California Gas and Electric Corporation.

Coleman, S. Waldo. b. Grass Valley 1882; d. Stanford, California, March 14, 1972. Son of John C. Coleman (one of 10 children). Graduate electrical engineer, University of California, Berkeley, 1903. President Coast Counties Light and Power Company 1912-28, at which time company was acquired by Standard Oil of California until sold to Pacific Gas and Electric Company. Coleman arranged merger of Coast Counties with San Benito Light and Power (1911) and took over gas and electric plants in Gilroy (1922). In 1914 he developed Contra Costa Gas Company as separate firm until merged in 1923 into Coast Counties. Coleman was president Santa Cruz Seaside Company 1915-28 and chief stockholder until its sale in 1946 to a group of Santa Cruzans.

Cooper, John L. b. Gettysburg, Pennsylvania, 1828; d. Santa Cruz January 6, 1887. To California May 1849; Santa Cruz 1851. With brother William, ran Cooper Brothers on Front Street for many years.

Cox, Edmund James. b. Australia; d. Santa Cruz January 29, 1895. Cashier Bank of Santa Cruz County 1874-86; to Los Angeles; to a bank in Tulare; returned to Santa Cruz 1894. Longtime Santa Cruz school trustee; member Los Angeles Board of Education.

Effey, William. b. Germany 1828; naturalized Davenport, Iowa, February 3, 1857; to Santa Cruz 1865. Jeweler, Pacific Avenue near Lincoln. Director Bank of Santa Cruz County 1877. Mayor Santa Cruz 1884.

Ely, William. b. Rome, New York, September 21, 1828. Woolen mill worker, Joliet, Illinois; to Placerville July 1850. Potato business failed 1852. Cattle business prospered. To Santa Cruz 1869. Farmer 1871. Capitalist and director Bank of Santa Cruz County 1877.

Ely, Frank William. b. Marin County, California, November 11, 1857. Son of William. Learned telegraphy as boy. Graduate San Jose business college. Baggagemaster, freight agent, conductor with Santa Cruz Railroad. Furniture business Pacific Avenue. To Paso Robles about 1899. In 1908 head salesman, Breuner's, Oakland.

Forgeus, James W. In July 1906 the *Surf* reviewed some of Forgeus' local accomplishments since coming to Santa Cruz from Kansas in 1899: "One of the first big deals made by Mr. Forgeus . . . was the selling of the Kerr property, which had lain idle for years, to F.W. Billing. In this about $50,000 was involved. Following that quickly was the purchase of the Big Creek Power Company from Fred Swanton and associates, in which Mr. Forgeus interested Messrs. Packard and Billing, who furnished the money to improve the big power plant up the coast, which is now worth fully half a million.

"The next transaction in which this Napoleon of finance figured was the development of the San Vincente Grant, of about 8,000 acres, which had lain idle for probably 35 years. He put new life and new capital into the Santa Cruz Lime Company until it now controls a practically inexhaustible supply of lime rock together with the finest timber supply in this portion of the state.

"Then came the sale of the Watsonville Light and Power Company . . . to Messrs. Martin and Lowe, who have added a splendid new power house and otherwise improved the property so that it is now worth fully $200,000. After this Mr. Forgeus bought the Santa Cruz Electric Railway. . . . Recently, with D.W.

Johnston, his real estate partner, he purchased the big Eckle ranch of several thousand acres in Colusa County, trading therefor in part payment a big slice of Wood's Lagoon waterfront in this city."

Forgeus was a director of the Big Creek Power Company in March 1900. He was manager of that company, and also the Santa Cruz Lime Company, in January 1902. In August 1908 his real estate firm was Forgeus, Johnston, and Burland.

Foster, Edward. b. Prussia 1840; to Santa Cruz 1865; naturalized Santa Cruz August 16, 1867. Blacksmith and carriage shop, Front Street.

Francis, Joseph. b. Portugal 1825; naturalized Santa Cruz April 21, 1862. Farmer 1866.

Granger, F.S. Incorporator, with James W. Rea of San Jose, of the San Jose, Saratoga, and Los Gatos Interurban Railroad Company, October 17, 1902. Vice-president in May 1903 when company was reincorporated as San Jose-Los Gatos Interurban Railway Company. Reportedly forced out April 9, 1904, when backers sold their interest to a new syndicate financed by the Southern Pacific. In July 1904 was a target, with Rea, of a lawsuit by H.K. Gilman of St. Louis alleging nonpayment of debts. Reported the *Sentinel:* "The complaint alleges that in April 1903, Rea and Granger, doing business as the Saratoga Construction Company, entered into a contract with the San Jose and Santa Clara Valley Railroad to construct the road; that afterward Rea and Granger entered into another contract, with the plaintiff, for the supplies to be sent and that the total amount used was $250,248.72 in value, and that of this sum only $201,961.30 was ever paid." Mr. Rea, when interviewed, called these supplies second-rate materials and threatened to have Mr. Gilman arrested if he ever sets foot in California, the *Sentinel* said.

In 1907 Granger briefly owned the Unique Theater on Pacific Avenue, Santa Cruz.

Greene, Edward C. b. St. Albans, Vermont, May 18, 1834. Elected to Vermont State Senate 1884. To Santa Cruz 1885. City councilman 1892-94. Associated with D. Younglove in Junction Mine near Grants Pass, Oregon, 1897. Residing in Palo Alto 1903.

Harrison, Cornelius Gooding. b. Illinois 1829. Mill owner San Jose 1867. Incorporator North Side Horse Railroad Company, San Jose, June 1875. Incorporator South East Side Horse Railroad, San Jose, March 1877. Major investor Peoples Horse Railroad Company, San Jose, March 1878.

Haslam, William Douglass. b. Santa Cruz October 3, 1860; father was Santa Cruz county clerk for eight years. Grocery clerk East Oakland, then bookkeeper City Bank and City Savings Bank. Cashier City Bank 1895-1901.

Hihn, Frederick Augustus. b. Holzminden, Germany, August 16, 1829; naturalized Santa Cruz July 2, 1855; d. Santa Cruz 1913. Grocery and general merchandising business. Investor March 1858 in Santa Cruz Turnpike Company building road from Soquel to San Jose (first wagon road over Santa Cruz Mountains to Santa Clara Valley). State assemblyman from Santa Cruz 1869. Laid out Camp Capitola 1869, changing name from La Playa de Soquel. President Santa Cruz Railroad 1873-81. Town trustee 1874. Developer Santa Cruz water system, using hollowed redwood logs. Helped establish Santa Cruz City Bank 1886 at Cooper and Pacific, serving as vice-president for about 20 years. Founded Hihn Company (real estate).

Hihn acquired George Otto's Soquel Sugar Works November 27, 1880, for $100 by sheriff's sale. In July 1897 he bought $10,000 Chace mansion (John R. Chace) for $25 plus $7,000 note to City Bank, upon Chace's bankruptcy. In April 1903 he bought equipment of old electric light works which had been stored in Monterey County and developed a lighting system for East Santa Cruz, Soquel, and Capitola.

Reportedly Hihn took $30,000 from his Santa Cruz grocery business and invested wisely in property, becoming a millionaire. Ernest Otto, writing in the *Sentinel* in June 1965, described the man and his accomplishments: "He was a California pioneer, a '49er and proud of being one. For years he headed the Society of

California Pioneers and for many years he annually entertained the entire group at a dinner, in the later years in the Hotel Capitola.

"He was a man who established industries. He founded Capitola, operated sawmills, and was about the largest property owner in the county. He owned a large part of the Soquel Augmentation Rancho, much of it covered with virgin timber. It was one of the old-time Spanish ranchos.

"Timber for his sawmills was cut from a vast forest of huge redwoods on this property. His largest sawmill was several miles back in the mountains from Aptos in a section known as Valencia. He had the Valencia mill along Valencia Creek, a beautiful stream which runs into Aptos Creek in Rio del Mar, then the Aptos rancho of Claus Spreckels, a short distance south of the Santa Cruz-Watsonville freeway.

"Valencia Creek had its mill dam. In the mill section was a village where employees of the mill resided. In the village was the Valencia hall, still a building in the section, where church services, dances and social gatherings were held.

"After the timber had been cut off, much of the forest property was sold to ranchers, and the land became one of the finest places in the county for the production of high-quality apples. Descendants of Hihn have orchards in the section to this day.

"The next mill was at Glenwood in the Santa Cruz Mountains where there was good rail transportation. Machinery from the Valencia mill was moved to Glenwood. These mills brought an industry within the Santa Cruz city limits as a planing mill operated on Washington Street in the city.

"The Hihn mills and the Loma Prieta mill made Aptos a lively village, especially on weekends.

"In the Hihn forests were the Hihn Sulphur Springs where many went for health-giving sulphur baths. These were below Loma Prieta and near what is now known as Highland Way. One crossed Soquel Creek 26 or 27 times in going up the beautiful gorge after leaving the Hinckley Creek section."

One intriguing story is that the Hihn fortune rested at least partly on the discovery of a huge boulder containing a large amount of gold. Hihn, who wore a gold nugget on his watch chain, never quashed the rumor which broke out in March 1895, causing some excitement and a minor flurry of prospecting. The supposed site was Gold Gulch, in the Ben Lomond area.

In 1920 California's state mineralogist investigated the rumor, reporting that the gulch indeed showed colors in almost any part of it. "Many years ago a boulder was discovered in this canyon from which was extracted $35,000 in gold," he declared. "Whether this boulder was broken from a lead in the immediate vicinity or whether ages ago it was broken from the Mother Lode in the Sierras and found its way here, is a question that has not yet been determined."

Hoffman, Christian. b. Germany 1836; naturalized by naturalization of his father. Teamster 1868. Director Bank of Santa Cruz County 1877. Realtor 1894. Republican candidate California State Senate, 27th District, May 1904.

Hotaling, Anson P. b. New York 1827; d. San Francisco February 16, 1900. Descendant of Henry Hudson, the Dutch explorer. To San Francisco 1852 around the Horn. Engaged briefly in mining, then in wholesale liquor business. Developed foreign trade, first to South Seas and Russian settlers on Amoor River, then 1877 to Australia. Mining interests. Substantial San Francisco real estate holdings, especially in Golden Gate Park area. In March 1887 completed Hotaling Block in Santa Cruz. Annual income reportedly $400,000 in 1891. President and chief subscriber Peoples Bank, Santa Cruz, January 1892. Investing heavily in beach improvements with Leibbrandt and Miller March 1893. Opened St. George Hotel, Pacific Avenue, June 1897.

Huntington, Henry E. b. Oneonta, New York, February 27, 1850; d. Philadelphia May 23, 1927, age 77. Nephew of Collis P. Huntington, co-founder Central Pacific and Southern Pacific railroads. In 1898 owned a San Francisco street railway; sold to buy into Los Angeles street railways and eventually formed the $100 million Pacific Electric, which he sold to the Southern Pacific. He retained his other major property, Los Angeles Railway, until his death. Huntington left estate of $7.5 million.

Irish, Harley E. To Santa Cruz from New York in late 1880s; established bookstore and stationery business. Director Bank of Santa Cruz County 1901. Heavy investor Santa Cruz Beach, Cottage, and Tent City Corporation 1903. With Henry Willey, heavy investor 1908 in Cottage City Investment Company, developers of Cottage City tract on East Cliff.

Jeter, William T. Attorney; mayor Santa Cruz 1892-94. Jeter and Makinney law offices. Appointed California lieutenant-governor October 1895 to fill unexpired term of Spencer G. Millard; served in that post until January 1899. Director Big Creek Power Company March 1900. President Bank of Santa Cruz County 1901, 1903.

Leibbrandt, John. b. Germany 1816. Naturalized Indiana March 7, 1843. Farmer 1866.

Logan, John Harvey. To Santa Cruz 1866 from San Jose where he was a protege of Judge C.T. Ryland. First judge Santa Cruz County Superior Court, serving until 1884. President Bank of Santa Cruz County. Reappointed Superior Court September 2, 1893. Instrumental about 1900 in developing community of Clear Creek (now Brookdale) in San Lorenzo Valley and in securing a state fish hatchery for that community.

In 1880 Judge Logan built a landmark residence on a hillside overlooking Monterey Bay and the former Santa Cruz Mission. Constructed of redwood, it featured an innovation: sheets of pressed, white-painted metal rather than wood siding nailed to the outside. Around the house were gardens where Logan, an avid horticulturist, developed in 1890 an unusual mammoth berry—a cross between a native blackberry sport (*Auginbaugh*) and the Red Antwerp raspberry. He sent samples to a firm in Portland, Oregon, and later marketed the berry, which gained widespread popularity. A March 1901 advertisement in the *Sentinel* extolled the virtues of the "mammoth blackberry developed by Judge Logan, grown at the Pajaro Nursery under exclusive propagating rights from Judge Logan." Eventually the berry was christened "loganberry" in honor of its discoverer.

Lukens, Evan. b. Pennsylvania 1834. Began as Front Street blacksmith and wheelwright working with Amner Foundry, River Street. Shop on Park Street, just east of Opera House, in May 1890.

Makinney, Hampton Emmett. b. Ohio 1842; to Santa Cruz 1866 from Placerville where he was a miner, schoolteacher. Teacher; principal; county superintendent of schools. Appointed county clerk December 1873. Notary public; searcher of records. Jeter and Makinney law offices 1894. H.E. Makinney and Sons, agents Santa Fe Railroad, 10 Cooper Street, 1894.

McLaughlin, Frank. b. New York 1855; d. Santa Cruz November 16, 1907. Mining speculator and promoter from Oroville. Noted for phenomenal physique. Became wealthy in mining. Built tavern Santa Cruz 1890. Helped promote Big Bend Power Company. Chairman California Republican Central Committee 1897 and manager of several state Republican political campaigns. Faced with vanished fortune, Major McLaughlin killed his daughter Agnes and committed suicide.

McQuigg, Martin V. Franchisee Monterey and Pacific Grove Railway (horsecar company) 1890. Banker Ontario, San Bernardino County, September 1902. Secretary Monterey and Pacific Grove, June 1903. President Monterey County Gas and Electric Company March 1905.

Otto, George. b. Prussia 1829; d. Santa Cruz December 14, 1899. To Santa Cruz 1853 from Baltimore. Merchant 1866. Proprietor Otto's Hall and Soquel Sugar Works. County treasurer August 1879. Arrested for misappropriating funds; found guilty May 1882 and sentenced to minimum one-year term California state prison.

Packard, John Q.A. b. New York; d. Santa Cruz October 1, 1908. To Marysville about 1878, then to Salt Lake City where he became wealthy from mining and mill enterprises. To Santa Cruz 1900 as co-purchaser (with F.W. Billing) Big Creek Power Com-

pany; engaged in ranching and electric power development. Major investor Ocean Shore Railroad. According to *Surf*, it was his money—$218,000—that bought the city property that was to become part of the road. Packard, who never married, reportedly left estate of $20 million.

Parker, Frank H. Pianos and organs. Real estate and loans 1892-1908.

Phelan, James Duval. b. San Francisco April 20, 1861; d. Saratoga (Montalvo), California, August 7, 1930. Graduate St. Ignatius College, San Francisco, 1881. Chairman Union Bank and Trust Company; director First National Bank and First Federal Trust Company, San Francisco. Mayor San Francisco; instrumental in bringing Hetch-Hetchy water to city. Regent University of California 1898-1914. U.S. Senator from California 1915-21. Following 1906 earthquake, President Theodore Roosevelt sent $10 million relief aid to Phelan personally rather than to San Francisco municipal government. Phelan died unmarried, willing Montalvo estate to San Francisco Art Association.

Pierce, James Pieronnet. b. Friendsville, Pennsylvania, August 25, 1825; d. Alameda, California, February 26, 1897. To San Francisco via Isthmus 1854. Miner Smartsville, Yuba County; became owner Blue Gravel Mine, later Excelsior Water and Mining Company; sold 1881. Bought country home (New Park), Santa Clara County, 1866. Moved to San Francisco 1868. About 1875, took over interest in seawall project on death of brother-in-law A.H. Houston, a financier of pioneering San Francisco and San Jose Railroad (1860). Bought Enterprise Mill (a small planing mill), Santa Clara, 1877, and changed name to Pacific Manufacturing Company, incorporated 1879. Bought timberland in Santa Cruz Mountains 1874-75; built mill at Ben Lomond. Founder Bank of Santa Clara County. Trustee Mills Seminary (later Mills College). Weathered bank failure May 1893 caused by misappropriation of funds by two employees.

Porter, Warren R. b. Santa Cruz March 30, 1861. Son of John T. Porter, organizer Bank of Watsonville and co-founder Loma Prieta Lumber Company. Graduated St. Augustine Military College 1880. Bank teller, then bookkeeper Loma Prieta Lumber Company 1884. Company secretary 1886. Incorporator and director Pajaro Valley National Bank, Watsonville, of which he was president 1900-22. California lieutenant-governor 1907-11.

Pray, Amasa. b. U.S. 1817. Merchant 1866.

Robinson, E.H. b. Maine. Co-founder Robinson and Cordes Real Estate, Pacific Avenue. Bought controlling interest Parker and Robinson hardware business January 1893. With son, bought Pavilion Feed Yard February 1894. President Board of Trustees, East Cliff Drive. Retired from real estate business May 1901. Suffering from cancer of right hand, had hand amputated above wrist January 1907.

Silent, Charles. b. Germany 1843; naturalized by naturalization of father, Ohio, 1854. Franchisee horse railroad, Santa Cruz County, March 1868. Incorporator San Jose and Santa Clara Railroad Company July 1868. First president Santa Cruz and Felton Rail Road Company. Appointed associate justice, Arizona Supreme Court, February 1878. Silent went to Long Beach in mid-1880s to become a land owner.

Simpson, John F. b. Maine; to Santa Cruz 1852. In April 1908 described as "venerable bachelor."

Smith, James Philip. Friend of Henry Morrison Flagler and President Theodore Roosevelt. With wife, former Susan Crooks, residing in Paris June 1904. Sizeable real estate holdings, Santa Cruz, January 1908.

Smith, R.C.P. Treasurer Monterey and Pacific Grove electric railway 1903, 1905.

Spreckels, Claus. b. Launstedt, Hannover, Germany, July 9, 1828; d. San Francisco 1908. Eldest of six children. To Charleston, South Carolina, 1848; opened grocery store and acquired lands. To New York City 1855; established wholesale and retail grocery business. To San Francisco by sea 1856. Bought and developed 2,390-acre Aptos Rancho, Santa Cruz County. Built sugar factory Watsonville 1887 that was later moved to community of

Spreckels a few miles south of Salinas in Monterey County.

Spreckels operated out of San Francisco, eventually from the Claus Spreckels Building (later Central Tower Building) at Third and Market. With other family members he founded a powerful combine—Western Sugar Refining Company—whose multiple interests included real estate, farms, and rail and water transportation. Charles M. Coleman, in his book *P.G. and E. of California*, describes Spreckels as a man of even temperament but fiercely determined when provoked. In 1899, he relates, the German took it as a personal affront when President Joseph B. Crockett of the San Francisco Gas and Electric Company, after several inquiries, lightly dismissed Spreckels' complaint that smoke from a powerhouse was blowing into his offices. So Spreckels organized the Independent Electric Light and Power Company to challenge Crockett's firm. A four-year feud ensued during which Crockett belatedly corrected the problem. Thus mollified, Spreckels sold out to Crockett in 1903.

Margaret Koch, in her book *Santa Cruz County: Parade of the Past*, provides the following contemporary description: "Claus Spreckels is of the German race, well preserved and active in his habits. Large-souled in all his numerous business operations. He is a busy man. His farm, hotel, sugar refinery in San Francisco, and large sugar plantation in the Sandwich Islands keep him constantly employed, yet he always has time for a kind word to all, whether rich or poor." In 1899 Spreckels loaned $25,000 to the state plus other funds to help destitute ranchers in southern Monterey County and northern San Luis Obispo County. Two years later he was seeking reimbursement from the state, all proceeds to go the University of California.

Swanton, Albion Paris. b. U.S. 1817 Livery keeper 1866. Building livery stable Lower Plaza, improving boarding house Mission Street, March 1880. County supervisor 1894.

Swanton, Fred Willer. b. Brooklyn, New York, April 11, 1862; d. Santa Cruz September 2, 1940. Son of A.P. Swanton. To Santa Cruz with parents 1866. Graduated Heald's Business College, San Francisco, 1881. Bookkeeper Centennial sawmill above Felton April 1882. Went into partnership with father 1883 to build three-story hotel on Front Street, at site of present Santa Cruz main post office. With father, also ran Bonner Stables adjacent to hotel. Both structures burned on Memorial Day 1888.

Opened Palace of Pharmacy 1888 on Pacific Avenue in IOOF Building but sold business following year. Briefly managed Opera House.

Started electric light business October 1889 in partnership with Dr. H.H. Clark. Promoted Santa Cruz's first electric railway 1891. Also promoted pioneering telephone company. Local agent Union Pacific Railroad November 1892. Organized Big Creek Power Company 1896, of which he was general manager. Sold company 1900; went briefly to Alaskan gold fields but returned to organize Santa Cruz Oil Company, which operated in Bakersfield area.

In 1903, with others, helped promote Capitola electric railway in competition with original street railway company. Also organized Santa Cruz Beach, Cottage, and Tent City Corporation October 1903 to build casino, pleasure pier, and tent city that opened in 1904 and burned in 1906. With John Martin and others, reorganized corporation as Santa Cruz Beach Company and built replacement casino—the structure existing today.

In 1908 Swanton and family incorporated as Swanton Investment Company to develop Swanton Beach Park subdivision on West Cliff Drive. This development failed and was deeded to the State of California as a state park. In 1910 promoted and built Casa del Rey Hotel on Beach Street opposite casino. The expense pushed Swanton into bankruptcy 1912.

Swanton helped organize the 1915 Panama-Pacific Exposition in San Francisco and, in 1916, tried to develop a chrome mine near Placerville. Mayor Santa Cruz 1927-33. Forced into bankruptcy a second time 1930, claiming debts of $57,000 and sole assets his $100 per month salary as mayor. He died almost penniless in 1940.

"He had created—and lived through—some of the greatest tourist development of that day," says Margaret Koch in her book *Santa Cruz County: Parade of the Past*. "He had lived through several lifetimes, right in Santa Cruz, all rolled into one short span. He was a developer *par excellence*—a promoter who got some great ideas and pushed them through."

Never was he more at his prime during the years 1903-07 when he was promoting his tent city and later the Neptune Casino, of which he was director-general. "Swanton began a publicity campaign for the City of Santa Cruz that has never been equalled. He talked the Southern Pacific into giving him a five-coach special train. Swanton loaded it with two brass bands, a bunch of Santa Cruz civic leaders and a goodly crew of advertising men.

"Arriving in a town, he would parade his bands up to the city hall, introduce Santa Cruz dignitaries to the host dignitaries, and exchange long and flowery speeches. In Sacramento and Marysville, the arrival of Swanton's special train was an event of sufficient importance to close the schools for the day!"

Similar fanfare attended the opening of the rebuilt casino in June 1907. Brass bands and the Royal Hawaiian Orchestra entertained. The special train of dignitaries this time included a military band, and there was a private bar for thirsty travelers. "Fred really believed in spreading the gospel. Oldtimers in the San Joaquin Valley used to refer to Santa Cruz as 'Swanta Cruz'."

Swift, Elias J. b. New York 1848; d. Santa Cruz February 1, 1889. To Santa Cruz 1878 from Salinas, where he managed Abbott House. Leased 150-room Pacific Ocean House. Bought Kittridge House March 1887.

Sylvar, Jackson. b. Portugal 1840; naturalized Santa Cruz August 13, 1867; d. January 1908. Saloon keeper 1867. Building commercial building corner Laurel and Pacific 1878. County undersheriff and jailer. Sold saloon 1888. As a young man, Captain Sylvar bought property on Sylvar Street facing Upper Plaza. Built home, which he sold to O.H. Bliss when his wife died. Business advisor to his countrymen in Santa Cruz. Large property holder. Large investor City Bank at initial incorporation.

Thurber, Isaac Lane. b. U.S. 1835. Stone cutter 1866. Building and road contractor. Building two-story tenement March 1877. Director Bank of Santa Cruz County 1881. Director City Bank March 1901.

Tisdale, William DeWitt. b. Utica, New York, October 12, 1845; d. Los Gatos, California, 1898. To California 1854. Attended Santa Clara College. Quartz miner Nevada County; returned to San Jose November 1871. Appointed cashier First National Bank of San Jose, later rose to become president. President Electric Improvement Company (San Jose). President San Jose Water Works.

Vahlberg, William T. b. Germany 1828; naturalized Yuba County, California, May 20, 1861. Baker in Santa Cruz 1866. Local newspaperman. Circulation manager, *Oakland Tribune*, 1907. Retired from newspaper work 1908 to take up real estate and mining stocks.

Wanzer, James Olin. b. New York City, September 16, 1837. To Santa Cruz 1862. Attorney; deputy county clerk 1864. Secretary Racing Association 1870-85.

Weeks, Thomas J. b. Kennebec County, Maine, December 22, 1829. To California 1849. Briefly a miner, then farming and real estate Santa Cruz.

Werner, John. b. Germany April 11, 1829; naturalized Santa Cruz July 23, 1858; d. Santa Cruz November 26, 1899. "Uncle John," as he was known locally, came to New York 1848; lived briefly in New York, Philadelphia, and South Macon, Georgia. Came to California 1852 and to Santa Cruz April 3, 1853. Saddler 1867. Established harness and saddlery business Santa Cruz. Retired about 1894. Accumulated local property holdings.

West, Edmund, Swift. b. Essex County, New York, May 2, 1837; to California 1851, to Santa Cruz 1863. Wharfman 1867. Wharf manager, California Powder Works, 1865-80. Retired from milk business October 1880; relocated to Casper, Mendecino County,

California. West and Thorvard employment agents, San Francisco, January 1883. Railroad construction superintendent, Southern Pacific, Monterey, October 1883. Santa Cruz agent for A.P. Hotaling 1894.

Willey, Henry. b. Vermont; came to Santa Cruz as young man about 1875 when uncle, Dr. S.H. Willey, was pastor Congregational Church. Hardware merchant, Pacific Avenue, 1891. First and only president People's Bank. City councilman 1903. In 1908, with Harley Irish, heavy investor Cottage City Investment Company, owners Cottage City tract on East Cliff.

Younger, Charles B. b. Liberty, Missouri, December 10, 1831. Attorney for F.A. Hihn in railroad and water-company matters.

Younglove, D. Investor pioneering Sacramento Electric Light Company that brought electric lighting to state capitol. With E.G. Greene, investor 1897 in Junction Mine near Grants Pass, Oregon.

Index

717565